A YOUR BODY,

MW01064209

your Emotions, Yourself

a guide to your changing emotions

Doreen L. Virtue, Ph.D.
Illustrations by Tanya Brokaw

Lowell House
Juvenile
Los Angeles

CONTEMPORARY BOOKS
Chicago

To my beautiful nieces,
Caryn, Candice, and Caitlin Hannan

Copyright © 1996 by RGA Publishing Group, Inc.
All rights reserved. No part of this work may be reproduced or transmitted in any form or by any means, electronic or mechanical, including photocopying and recording, or by any information storage or retrieval system, except as may be expressly permitted by the 1976 Copyright Act or in writing by the publisher.

Publisher: Jack Artenstein
Associate Publisher, Juvenile Division: Elizabeth Amos
Director of Publishing Services: Rena Copperman
Editor in Chief, Juvenile Nonfiction: Amy Downing
Managing Editor, Juvenile Division: Lindsey Hay
Art Director: Lisa Theresa Lenthall
Interior Design: Brenda Leach / Once Upon a Design
Cover Photograph: Ann Bogart
Cover Model: Katie Meledy, age 12

Library of Congress Catalog Card Number: 96-35883

ISBN: 1-56565-534-6

Lowell House books can be purchased at special discounts when ordered in bulk for premiums and special sales. Contact Department JH at the following address:

Lowell House Juvenile
2020 Avenue of the Stars, Suite 300
Los Angeles, CA 90067

Manufactured in the United States of America

10   9   8   7   6   5   4   3   2   1

Contents

Your Emotions, Yourself will clear up a lot of questions you have about your feelings and about growing up. However, no book can answer every question you might have as you enter your teen years. If you have a question you need answered, don't be afraid to talk to an adult about it—especially your mom or dad! You may even want to sit down with a parent and read through parts of this book together.

This book is not intended to treat, diagnose, or prescribe. If you or anyone else feels you have a serious emotional difficulty, consult a licensed psychological counselor.

"*A*m I Normal to Feel This Way?"

Sometimes I think everybody but me knows some secret about life. It just seems like everyone's so happy, but I'm all mixed up and scared.

— Tiffany Marks, age 12, Hendersonville, Tennessee

*S*ometimes life seems so complex. No one understands you. In fact, you can barely understand yourself! One minute you're excited, and the next moment you're bored. Some days you're happy, while other days every little thing gets on your nerves.

What gives?

Your emotions, that's what. And just as your body is beginning to go through some major changes, so too are your emotions. Some of these mood swings are purely based upon your body's changes due to puberty. Still other emotions are triggered by the ever increasing pressures you're encountering.

After all, you've got an awful lot to think about: school,

boys, family, gym class, tests, clothes and makeup, and friendships. On top of all that, you're getting pressure from some adults to start making plans about your future. Your head is spinning with all these decisions and choices.

At times, you may wish you could return to being a six-year-old when life seemed a lot simpler.

> **Back then, your biggest worry was which *dress* to put on your *Barbie* or if you had enough legos to build your own fort.**

But let's face it: Even though things seem a bit complex right now, deep down you know you're headed for some excitement in the coming years.

Your occasional feelings of confusion or self-doubt are perfectly normal, as are all emotions you experience. Everybody goes through ups and downs—even teachers! Some people are just careful to always conceal what they're feeling.

Your Emotions, Yourself explains some of the more confusing feelings that you've no doubt experienced. You'll learn the whys, hows, and whats of your inside self. In addition, you'll read about ways to deal with and lessen some of the more painful emotions. And you'll learn the signs indicating whether you, or someone you know, could benefit from an appointment with a professional counselor.

I hope you'll refer to *Your Emotions, Yourself* frequently for guidance to get you through life's rough spots and to cheer you on during its high points. After reading this book, you'll probably have a deeper appreciation for how wonderfully normal—and yet incredibly special—you are.

Enjoy!

Doreen Virtue, Ph.D.

CHAPTER 1

"What Are Emotions?"

I think that when you grow up, you stop having so many problems. It just seems like kids are the ones who have all the worries, like homework, grades, and stuff. What do adults have to worry about?

—April McMullen, age 11, Bloomington, Minnesota

Sometimes it seems hard to believe, but it's true: *everybody* has feelings! Even those adults who seem always under control, or those cool kids at school who don't show an ounce of concern or worry. Deep inside all of us are feelings that influence how we think and how we act twenty-four hours a day.

Emotions are a combination of thoughts, judgments, beliefs, and physical reactions to a given situation. For example, let's say you're in front of the class reading your report. You may experience the emotion "nervousness," which is a combination of these reactions:

- **your thoughts:** "I'll talk fast so I can get this over with!"

- **your judgment:** "This is a horrible situation. I just know everyone is laughing at me."

- **your beliefs:** "I worked hard on this paper, so I definitely deserve an 'A.'"

- **your physical reactions:** Rapid heartbeat, sweaty palms, dry throat, red face, and difficulty concentrating.

Extremely intense thoughts, judgments, beliefs, and physical reactions, as in this example, are your strong feelings. While many people feel nervous speaking to a group, some *love* an audience. These spotlight-lovers, in the same classroom situation, would experience a different set of strong feelings.

Here's another example: A girl in your class named Jasmine—who enjoys getting attention—is reading her paper outloud. Here's what may be going through her head and body:

- **Jasmine's thoughts:** "I'll tell them my newest joke, and really get them laughing."

- **Jasmine's judgments:** "This is so cool! I tell great jokes."

- **Jasmine's beliefs:** "Someday, I'll be a famous comedienne."

- **Jasmine's physical reactions:** Heartbeat slightly accelerated.

Excitement and nervousness may seem similar, but there is one major difference. Most people consider excitement a pleasant or positive emotion, while nervousness is considered an unpleasant, negative emotion.

Most of the time, you probably aren't aware of the feelings you're experiencing. It's usually just the strong emotions that get your attention. Have you recently experienced any of these emotional situations?

- ✿ A ***romantic crush*** on a really cute guy.

- ✿ ***Stress*** or ***pressure*** about your school grades.

- ✿ ***Loneliness*** when you were all alone.

- ✿ ***Frustration*** when your mom or dad told you, "No."

- ✿ ***Frightened*** by a scary movie.

- ✿ ***Worried*** that your pet was lost.

- ✿ ***Thrilled*** at the sight of an unexpected gift meant for you!

- ✿ ***Relieved*** when your report card showed decent grades.

These are all some heavy-duty emotions you've experienced. Throughout this book, you'll understand why you have certain feelings. You'll also learn ways to experience fewer negative emotions and more positive emotions.

Your *Right* to Have Emotions

Before you read another word, there are two important things for you to know. The first is that you have the right to feel any emotion that occurs. **Don't allow anyone to tell you that you shouldn't feel a certain way.** Whatever emotions you have are occurring for a good reason.

JOURNAL WRITING
POURING YOUR HEART OUT ON PAPER

Imagine writing a paper where neatness, spelling, punctuation, and grammar don't count! Journal writing is just such a no-rules-apply activity. But even more, **journaling** reduces confusion, anxiety, and depression. Writing in a journal is similar to keeping a diary, with one main difference. A diary is kept to record day-to-day events, while a journal is simply a collection of written-down feelings and thoughts. In journaling, all that matters is complete honesty with yourself about what you feel. It doesn't matter if you use a pen or a pencil, if you cross out words, or doodle on the edges.

You may want to purchase a cloth-covered blank book, or use a blank notepad reserved especially for your journal.

Some people write such private thoughts in their journal, they throw away each entry after they're done, while others keep the journal as a permanent record. It's interesting to read one's old journal entries to recognize recurring patterns or to see how far you've grown as a person. If you don't want others to read your thoughts, keep your journal in a private place.

Take a moment right now to give journaling a try firsthand. Grab some paper and a pen or pencil. You'll probably want to sit somewhere private and quiet. As you write, let your feelings flow, uncensored, and unedited.

Ready? Think of a recent situation that has affected you,

either positively or negatively. Write a sentence or two about your feelings, describing the incident in as much detail as you can remember.

Next, spend a moment writing how and why you might be feeling the way you do. See if you can untangle or pinpoint any other thoughts or feelings.

Write about any solutions or different points of view that occur to you as you're journaling.

In fact, if you deny having an emotion, it usually grows stronger. Have you ever tried to fight being embarrassed, for example? Perhaps you've noticed that this tactic only makes your face turn more red. But if, instead, you admitted the truth to yourself or someone else, the feelings of embarrassment would go away!

Second, certain emotions are shared by most people in similar situations, such as feeling sad over the death of a loved one, or feeling excited when you're opening a birthday gift. Some emotions are designed to warn you when trouble is brewing, such as the gut feelings you get when you meet a person who's not very nice. Still, other emotions are deeply personal, as with the sweet feelings only you get when you listen to a certain song that reminds you of a special person or event.

Personality Styles

You've probably noticed that all the kids and adults you meet have different ways of talking, behaving, and joking around. Think of a popular girl at school, and you'll likely recall her speaking mannerisms, her sense of humor, or the radiant way she smiles at everyone. These collective character traits make up a "personality." Personalities and emotions go hand in hand, because our personalities influence many of the feelings we experience. For instance, if you are easygoing, you may have a hard time getting angry about anything.

Some personality characteristics change as we get older, and others stay pretty much the same throughout our lifetime. That is, your outgoing twelve-year-old cousin will probably be a very friendly and talkative adult, but her hyper-energetic style may tone down as she gets older. The same is true about your own personality. Many of your present personality traits—whether you're funny, serious, romantic, or creative—will accompany you into adulthood. Other traits will disappear through your conscious decisions, maturing outlook, changed lifestyle habits, or accumulated experiences.

WHAT'S YOUR PERSONALITY STYLE?

How would you describe yourself? This is one quiz where there are no right, wrong, or best answers. The only thing that counts is honesty! Check all the words that apply to how you see yourself (or ask your best friend to help in picking which words best suit you):

___ Easygoing	___ Energetic	___ Serious	___ Funny
___ Talkative	___ Quiet	___ Curious	___ Polite
___ Sensitive	___ Shy	___ Outgoing	___ Friendly
___ Mischievous	___ Casual	___ Elegant	___ Imaginative
___ Creative	___ Romantic	___ Dramatic	___ Dependable
___ Helpful	___ Cautious	___ Proud	___ Kind
___ Bold	___ Loyal	___ Trend-setting	

Learning about your personality style is an important part of growing up for several reasons. First, it helps you to know yourself better so that you can predict how you'll react to people and situations. For example, if you know you are sensitive and quiet, you'll understand why you sometimes have a hard time dealing with loud and boisterous personality types. Second, by taking this quiz, you might decide to focus your energy on strengthening some of your personality traits, while minimizing others. In other words, you can custom-tailor your traits to suit the kind of person you want to be. Finally, and best of all, when you are more aware of your personality style, your **self-esteem** will rise as you accept how uniquely special you are.

Learning about yourself is a first step toward *liking* who you really are!

Where Do Emotions Come From?

Scientists who study emotions and personality come from a variety of academic fields, including medicine, psychology, and sociology. These experts often disagree about the source of feelings and personality. Their opinions form four different schools of thought.

The first school of thought is called "cognitive psychology." These psychologists believe feelings originate from peoples' thoughts and beliefs. They theorize that emotions such as **depression** are caused by thinking depressing thoughts. Cognitive psychologists teach people to choose happier thoughts in order to feel happier.

The second school of thought, "neuropsychiatry," focuses more on body functions such as **hormones** and brain chemistry. These scientists believe that our eating, sleeping, drinking, and exercise habits determine our emotional states. Therefore, by getting enough sleep, eating healthfully, and exercising regularly, we can feel happier.

Still other scientists believe our emotional patterns are influenced by our families through genetic heredity. This is called the "nature theory." Some doctors think we genetically inherit emotional traits such as depression or **anxiety.** This is partially supported by studies that show depression and some mental illnesses tend to run in families and twins.

The fourth school of thought concludes that we learn our emotional responses by watching how our parents react to different situations (for example, adopting Mom's habit of feeling stressed out in crowds). This is called "modeling" or the "nurture theory." For years, scientists have argued whether nature or nurture plays a bigger part in creating our emotional makeup.

What's your opinion?

You **CAN Deal With It!**

In your journal, write down three emotions you've experienced in the past week. Describe each situation that brought on the emotional response. If any of the emotions were negative, write how you could have responded to the situation with a more positive emotion.

CHAPTER 2

"Why Are My Emotions Changing?"

I used to be happy all the time, but lately it seems my brother and some of the kids at school really get on my nerves. I don't know why. Maybe they've changed, or maybe it's me. Whatever; I just know life is harder now.

—Nicole Adams, age 13, Carlsbad, California

Have you noticed that the closer you get to the teen years, the more emotional you become? If so, you're aware of one signal that the puberty process is upon you. Remember from chapter 1 those scientists who claim that the body's hormones are responsible for our emotional states? Well, many of your roller-coaster emotions are influenced by physical changes during adolescence.

As your body prepares for menstruation and eventual childbirth, your internal organs must produce substances called hormones. You'll read more about hormonal influences upon emotions later in the book. But for now, isn't it a relief to know that chemical changes in your body are one reason why you get *doubly* irritated at your sister's pranks these days? As your body gets used to the changes in hormones, your emotions will also even out.

In the Mood Swing

The whirlwind of changes you're experiencing leads to feeling a wide variety of emotions from day to day. On Monday, you're bored. On Tuesday, you're silly and can't stop laughing. On Wednesday, you're irritable. And on Thursday, you're bored again. *And on top of everything else, your little brother is calling you "moody"!*

Up and down emotions are called "mood swings." This is all perfectly normal during puberty, especially during stressful events such as family fights, final exams, or moving to a new home.

However, while your emotions may feel out of control, you still need to retain responsibility for your actions.

If you feel like taking your sister's makeup and "painting" her favorite blouse with it, *you* are making a choice to hurt her or not. And if you take the more aggressive route and ruin her shirt, you must accept the consequences.

Leave Me Alone . . . Please!

As you mature, you may want to pull away from your family and spend more time alone or with friends. Sometimes, you'd rather hang out with your buddies than take a family outing to the park. This is perfectly normal!

The human growth process occurs in stages. Adolescence is one stage, filled with tasks that prepare you for adulthood. One such task is called **separation-individuation**—the process of becoming a self-sufficient person. As you go through separation-individuation, you will prefer to spend more and more time away from your parents, which prepares you to eventually live away from home.

Though this task can feel painful at times both for you as well as for your parents, it is vital! If you don't learn how to make decisions for yourself, you won't become an independent adult.

Sometimes you'll feel in the middle of a tug-of-war between your friends and your folks, with both wanting your time and attention. Instead of getting stressed over time pressures, allow time with your friends, with your folks, and by yourself.

"Mom, That's So Embarrassing!"

Another change you may notice is that you begin to feel very self-conscious about your parents and how they act. You're horrified when your mom tries to hold your hand in public. Or, when your dad insists on meeting your guy friends. Or what about that time when your mother wore hair curlers when she picked you up from school. How could she?!

This self-consciousness is another normal part of breaking away from childhood. As children, we usually think of our parents as being perfect super-humans. But as you become an independent adult, you begin to notice that your parents are actually real-life human beings—complete with everyday people "flaws."

Reduce your embarrassment by remembering that every kid at school suffers from the same sort of worry that his or her parents are dorky or weird. Most people will not judge you because of something your parents do or don't do. And if they do make fun of your parents, they obviously aren't your friends in the first place.

In the meantime, try to bite your lip when you feel like criticizing your mom's outfit or your dad's taste in music. Just as you want people to respect what you like and dislike, adults feel the same way.

Life Is Change

Sometimes life seems like such a bummer! But don't despair! The parts of your life that feel awkward or painful will soon smooth out, so don't think that today's turmoil will last forever.

Some people have more difficulty coping with change than do others. But since change is an inevitable part of life, it's best to learn to go with the flow as best you can. Look at it this way, if you are happy with the changes going on in your life, enjoy them while you can. They won't last forever. Likewise, if you're miserable with a change, remind yourself that it won't last forever, either.

Now is a good time to learn how to ride out the changes of your life, maybe even with a sense of humor. Everyone experiences changes throughout his or her life. You can think right now how you'll answer these important questions: "How will I deal with life changes? Will I fight them? Will I welcome them? Or will I just try to ride them out?" Each situation you face demands its own response. Sometimes you will need to fight it, and other changes will be easier for you to accept.

You Are in Charge of Your Feelings

✦ "He made me so angry!"

✦ "She makes me feel very happy."

✦ "If it weren't for my little brother, I'd be perfectly content."

✦ "That guy really put me in a bad mood!"

How often have you heard someone make one of these comments or said something similar yourself? We often believe that other people "make" us feel a certain way. But the truth is that there is only one person who can make you feel an emotion: YOU!

"But what about when I'm around that irritating girl in my math class or my crabby science teacher?" your mind may argue.

While we definitely are influenced—positively and negatively—by the people around us, we still can exert some control and influence over our emotions.

... there is only one person who can make you feel an emotion:

Your thoughts and beliefs can determine how you feel about any given person or situation. For example, your mother scolds you because your room is messy. Do you feel:

1. *Peeved!* How could your mom be sooo mean?

2. **Guilty.** How could you let your room get so messy and let your mom down?

3. *STRESSED.* Not only do you have to clean your room, but you have to study for those two tests and baby-sit the neighbor kid. How can you do it all??

4. Confident. Everybody goofs up now and then, and you know that if you always keep your room clean, peace will reign in the house—and you'll feel better, too!

Depending on how you think about the situation, you may allow outside circumstances or people to control your emotions, as in examples 1 through 3.

Do you need to take more control over your feelings?

You CAN Deal With It!

You just get used to your life and activities, and all of a sudden—change! You get a new baby sister, your best friend is moving, or maybe you just started piano lessons and hey, practice takes up way more time than you thought!

Think about one change in your life that you will deal with in the next year or so. Will you welcome it or fight it? How will the change positively affect you?

CHAPTER 3

"Will the Real Me Please Stand Up?" Your Changing Self-Image

I always hear people saying that you should just be yourself. But I don't really know what that means.

— Bridget Doman, age 12, Walnut Grove, Missouri

Just as your emotions change like colors in a kaleidoscope, so do your self-image and self-esteem. These changes are a product of growing older, and in many ways, everyone goes through similar changes at roughly the same age. Psychologists call these age-related changes "life stages." Each stage builds up your emotional growth and develops your personal identity. (However, sometimes an unresolved life trauma or very low self-esteem can "stunt" your growth from stage to stage.)

As you read earlier, separating from your parents is a

normal part of growing up. Another major task of the adolescence stage is "finding an identity."

> *The most important part of your identity is a positive viewpoint about yourself. Liking who you are (which is not the same as being stuck-up, as you'll read) is important to developing healthy self-esteem.*

You've probably heard people talk about self-esteem, but what is it? It basically means how you feel about yourself. Healthy self-esteem means that you respect yourself, like yourself, know what your likes and dislikes are, and that you stand up for your rights.

People with healthy self-esteem are usually well-liked and respected by others. Several studies have concluded that people with high self-esteem usually have good social skills. Their social skills, in turn, attract lots of friends. It's unclear, however, which came first: the social skills or the self-esteem. Regardless, these studies do point to the value of developing a healthy attitude about yourself to hold on to throughout your life!

Studies about Self-Esteem

Researchers at Harvard University and the University of California, Berkeley, as well as the American Association of

University Women (AAUW) have given the area of self-esteem much attention during the 1990s. In particular, they have studied differences of self-esteem levels between boys and girls at a variety of ages.

Researchers found what a lot of females have long suspected: **Girls generally hold lower opinions about themselves than do boys.** More important though, these researchers noted the relationship of age to self-esteem. Until age twelve or thirteen, boys and girls have almost equal levels of healthy self-esteem. But just as girls are about to enter adolescence, **BOOM!** Their self-esteem drops radically below that of boys. For most girls, this self-esteem level never recovers to its former level.

From age fourteen to twenty-three, almost fifty percent of girls show significant drops in self-esteem. Only twenty percent of girls this age experience an increase in self-esteem. Boys in this same age group have very different self-esteem shifts: Just twenty percent drop in self-esteem, while a full thirty-three percent actually gain higher self-esteem, reports the University of California, Berkeley, in research done in 1993.

In 1991, according to the AAUW, evidence of this self-esteem gender gap shows up in the different ways boys and girls describe themselves. Girls between the ages of nine and fifteen are much more likely than boys of the same age to say they don't have enough talent or intelligence to achieve their life goals. Boys are twice as likely as girls to list their talents as the things they most like about themselves. In contrast, girls are more likely to say some aspect of their physical appearance is what is best about them.

LOW SELF-ESTEEM
What is low self-esteem?

Low self-esteem is when you have a low opinion of your-self, such as feeling as if you're going to get bad grades in school no matter how hard you study. Feelings of incompetence like this are really hurt-ful, because if you believe you are bound to fail, then you probably won't try very hard to succeed. By giving up before you've even started, you're bound to get dismal results. Then, your self-esteem takes even more of a nose dive, and you're scared to tackle the next challenge!

> ...if you believe you are bound to fail, **then you probably won't try very hard to succeed.**

Another destructive aspect of low self-esteem is when girls think that they are only valued for the way they look, instead of for who they are on the inside. Girls with **eating disorders** often feel this way. These girls believe that the only way they'll receive love and popularity is through attaining an unrealistically low body weight.

A person with low self-esteem feels unworthy of respect or love. She fears being rejected if others knew her true thoughts and feelings. So, instead of being *authentic* (her real self), she seeks reassurance of her self-worth in one of these three inef-fective ways:

1. **Unassertiveness** *(or passiveness)*: This is when some-one allows others to manipulate or take advantage of her. She is afraid that if she stands up for herself, something

bad will happen, such as being rejected, teased, yelled at, or punished.

For example, Danielle really wanted to be friends with pretty, popular Nicole. But Nicole treated her like a second-class citizen, always ordering Danielle around or making fun of her. Even though this behavior hurt Danielle's feelings, she held in her hurt in order to win Nicole's approval. Therefore, Nicole kept treating her badly, and Danielle never got the respect she deserved. As a result, Danielle's self-esteem plunged further. Had Danielle spoken up for herself, she'd feel better about herself and her self-esteem would rise, whether or not Nicole treated her differently.

2. **Passive-Aggressiveness:** A person says "yes" when she'd rather say "no." But even though she agrees to do something, the passive-aggressive person's actions will reveal her true wishes. She will either "forget" to perform the task, do it wrong, or she'll be too late per-forming it. This person is afraid that others will reject her if she's honest and tells them "no" in the first place. However, it's more likely that people snub her because they think she's wishy-washy.

Look at this example of what happened between two good friends. Linda asked if she could borrow Renee's expen-sive new sweater. Renee didn't want to lend her sweater to anyone, fearing that it would be stretched out, soiled, or otherwise ruined. But she feared losing Linda's friendship if she said "no." So, Renee agreed. Instead of leveling with Linda about her true feelings, Renee offered an excuse every day as to why she "forgot" to bring the sweater. Finally, Linda quit asking, but deep inside she wondered about Renee's behavior. Renee's passive-aggressive behavior had created a barrier between the two friends.

3. **Aggressiveness:** This is when someone bullies others in order to get her way. She's loud, foul-mouthed, and she may use physical force or tattle to adults to get what she wants. Who would ever guess that underneath that gruff exterior is someone who is scared to death of rejection? Yet, it's true: The truly secure person never needs to throw her weight around in order to get her way.

Carla was a big, strong girl with a hearty laugh. As captain of the softball team, she held a lot of clout during P.E. class. She could bark orders at the girls on the team, and everyone would obey. Carla was bossy off the baseball diamond, as well. If someone got upset at her joking, Carla would berate them with a "I was just kidding, you baby! You're too sensitive!"

Carla's loud domineering style covered the fact that she was lonely and suffered from low self-esteem.

HEALING LOW SELF-ESTEEM

Many people have low self-esteem, and everyone has behaved unassertively, passive-aggressively, or aggressively at one time or another. The good news is that low self-esteem is not a prison sentence; it's something you can fix! But just as maintaining body fitness requires regular exercise, so does your self-esteem!

Psychologists offer this advice for keeping self-esteem at healthy, high levels:

1. ***Take excellent care of yourself.*** When your body feels rested and fit, it's much easier to feel good about your life. Self-esteem stays high easier when you get enough rest, exercise, and eat a balanced diet.

2. ***Make time for fun.*** You work hard at school, and need some emotional rewards and relief from stress. Play, laughter, and friendship are essential to happiness and a high self-esteem. Balancing and scheduling schoolwork with enough time for play is a must for staying positive and excited about life.

3. ***Practice honesty.*** Self-esteem refers to the reputation you have with your own self. If you are untruthful, you will naturally think less highly about yourself.

4. ***Have goals.*** Know what you want and then take steps to achieve it. Research shows that people who set goals are among the highest achievers. Even the accomplishment of a small goal will give your self-esteem a big boost.

5. ***Take a stand.*** Be willing to defend your beliefs, opinions, and rights in ways that don't compromise other people's feelings or rights. (This is called **assertiveness**.)

You will feel proud of yourself, which automatically increases your self-respect and self-esteem.

ASSERTIVENESS: KEY TO HEALTHY SELF-ESTEEM

A person with healthy self-esteem is naturally likeable. She exudes a warmth, caring, and confidence that is irresistible to others. No wonder, then, that studies find people with high self-esteem are lonely less often than people with low self-esteem. How can you develop and maintain high self-esteem?

<u>**Be assertive!**</u> Just as unassertiveness, passive-aggressiveness, and aggressiveness are "styles" of communication, so, too, is assertiveness.

Many people mistake "assertiveness" for "aggressiveness." But they're not the same at all! Assertive behavior is when you are honest, while respecting your own rights and the rights of others. Aggressive behavior is when you show no respect for others' feelings.

Take a look at four friends, Molly, Kristy, Heather, and Brooke. They each have a different way of communicating, one more effective than the others. Can you figure out which one?

The girls wanted to go to the movies. Molly wanted to see the comedy, Kristy preferred the action flick, Heather wished to see the cartoon movie, and Brooke really preferred the romantic film.

Molly explained why she preferred the funny film, pointing out the great reviews it had received. Molly said she'd like to hold a vote among the four friends, with the majority ruling.

Kristy loudly told everyone they were sissies for wanting to see non-action movies. She also threatened to quit being their friend if she didn't get her way.

Heather didn't say anything. Instead, she kept her true wishes to herself.

Brooke loudly sighed, saying she'd go along with whatever the others wanted. But she also announced that there was a chance she'd be too busy to go to the movies.

Which girl acted assertively? Aggressively? Unassertively? Passive-aggressively?

Molly behaved assertively, because she showed respect for her own opinion, as well as for those around her. Kristy acted aggressively, trying to bully the others to get her own way. Heather was unassertive because she kept silent. Brooke behaved passive-aggressively, pretending to agree, but behaving in the opposite way.

How would you have acted?

"How Do I Look?" Your Body Image

Your feelings about your inner and outer self are changing in so many ways as you move into young adulthood! Your concerns about your outer self, including your weight, breasts, clothing, hair, and face, is called your "**body image**." How

do those concerns affect how you feel about yourself?

Surveys consistently show that ninety to ninety-eight percent of American females say they are "too fat." If you've just checked out the latest *TEEN* magazine, filled with superthin bodies, or turned on the TV to see beautiful, skinny figures sipping cappuccino from oversized cups, it's easy to see why so many girls feel they can't measure up. But that's not real life. If your weight concerns stem from unrealistic comparisons in magazines or on TV, think again.

and, if you are freaking out about your **growing breasts** and **rounding hips,** *don't forget* it's all a part of growing up, now, isn't it?

FASHION-CONSCIOUSNESS

Have you ever felt like school was a fashion show, or worse, like a fashion *contest?* And the most popular girls always wear the latest styles and own the most expensive shoes? You're not alone if you've felt pressure to dress or look a certain way. Rest assured that the other kids at school are experiencing similar confusion about how wardrobes affect popularity.

Some girls play it safe with fashion choices by dressing similarly to what their friends are wearing. They ask one another what they are going to wear. This tendency to coordinate fashions with one's friends continues throughout life for some women. Maybe you've even overheard your mom ask her friend what she plans to wear to certain events! This is okay, as long as you feel comfy in what you are wearing.

The important thing is that your wardrobe reflects and expresses who you are as a person, not the current fashion trend. You look your best in clothes that are comfortable and that suit your personality and lifestyle. If you buy and wear an uncomfortable but trendy outfit in an effort to fit in, you won't be happy. No matter how fashionable your outfit, if you look unhappy, you won't look—or feel—your best.

LOOKING GOOD ON A BUDGET

Looking good means a lot more than simply wearing the right clothes for you. This is a relief since most of us don't have a limitless cash flow to keep up with the latest styles.

Instead, focus on taking care of your body: regular bathing (with soap, and at least every other day), and keeping your hair clean and neatly styled.

In the end, who you are *inside* counts more than how you dress or look on the outside. However—let's be real here—people do make snap judgments about us based upon our appearances. It's part of being human, and you probably do it yourself. So why not make life a little bit easier on yourself and take time to be and stay appropriately groomed? It's all a part of taking good care of yourself, which always boosts your self-esteem.

BODY IMAGE AND WANTING TO LOOK OLDER

Sometimes you may feel self-conscious because you wish you felt or looked older than your age. Perhaps the other girls at school are wearing bras or makeup, and you want to, too— but you're unsure how to approach your mother about the topic. Or, maybe you wish your body was shaped like the older girls, so you could impress that cute guy in fifth period.

It's common for girls your age to compare one another's bodies, and to sometimes make comments about the differences. You may feel like your body is unlike anybody else's. And guess what—you're right! That's the great thing about you—you're unique—and so is everyone.

Your body image concerns become even more tangled if you negatively compare your looks against other girls you see at school or the underwear models in magazines. For example, you may wish your breasts were larger, or wish you could wear a bra when you don't really need one. These are normal feelings!

Females have many emotions tied into body-image concerns. Among these concerns are questions such as, "When can I shave my legs?" and "What happens to my body when I begin having a period?" All these questions are best answered by a trusted adult, such as a parent, family doctor, or school nurse. These deeply personal body image concerns about your weight, breasts, clothing, or hair, may feel awkward—even embarrassing!—but if you remember that every guy and girl has similar feelings, you'll feel less alone.

You CAN Deal With It!

Think about how you communicate with others. What's the communication style you use to get your message across? Is it effective?

CHAPTER 4

Your Body and Emotions

The first time I had my period, I was scared because I thought I had cut myself. It was embarrassing to tell my mom about the blood because of where it was and all that. But I'm glad I did, because she explained a lot to me. Then I wasn't scared any more.

— Melody Hansen, age 14, Lake Oswego, Oregon

Many of your changing emotions are triggered by the changes your body is experiencing or is about to experience. After all, you're no longer a little girl. You're well on your way toward becoming a woman!

One of the ways your body is preparing for womanhood involves hormones. These chemicals in the brain and bloodstream influence many body functions, including menstruation, pregnancy, sexual arousal, energy, and even your appetite for food. Some of the shifts in your moods can be explained by the increase in hormones in your body. It's as if someone's been pouring mood-altering chemicals into your body—of course, it's going to affect you!

Crying spells, listlessness, indecisiveness, sudden anger flashes, and a new-found interest in boys are among the emotions that your hormones have been intensifying recently.

Even before you actually begin to have a period, your emotions have been affected by these bubbling brews of brain chemicals.

Your Period and Your Emotions

Many girls feel slightly depressed or irritable a couple of days before their period begins. The collection of emotional and physical changes that occur during the week before the period starts is called **premenstrual syndrome,** or PMS. Some girls never experience PMS at all, while a few are bedridden because their symptoms are so severe. Most girls are somewhere in the middle, experiencing minor changes or inconveniences right before their periods begin.

PMS symptoms include physical changes such as tender breasts and cramping. The emotional symptoms can be feelings of depression, irritability, fatigue, or anger without any cause. Some of these emotions are results of the physical pain associated with menstruation. Of course, you're more likely to be in a bad mood if your body hurts!

You can reduce or eliminate PMS symptoms by eating a low-fat, low-salt diet full of fresh fruits and vegetables, whole grain breads, and lots of fresh water. Avoid caffeine (like colas, chocolate, or coffee) and salty or sugary snack foods—these

substances play havoc with your hormones, which in turn increases PMS symptoms.

Aerobic exercise also improves your mood during the premenstrual phase of your menses, or period, and lowers stress levels. In fact, doctors recommend avoiding any unnecessary stress during the week before your period (in other words, make sure you study for that math test well before 11 P.M. the night before!). Finally, the advice your mother may have given holds true for reducing PMS symptoms: Get lots of sunshine, fresh air, and a good night's sleep.

PMS-PROOF FOODS

PMS often triggers cravings for sweet or salty foods that, unfortunately, only make the other PMS symptoms (like bloating, mood swings, and irritability) grow worse! One way to deal with PMS-triggered food cravings is to make healthy substitutes for empty-calorie foods, which will promote energy and stabilize moods.

INSTEAD OF	EAT
Chocolate candy bar	Fruit-sweetened granola bar
Ice cream	Fruit-sweetened yogurt
Potato chips	Air-popped popcorn without salt
French fries	Baked potato

MYTHS AND FACTS ABOUT PMS

Myth #1: *Every female has premenstrual syndrome.*

The Truth: While many suffer from PMS, others experience only slight or no symptoms.

Myth #2: *The only solution for PMS is an over-the-counter medication, such as Midol.*

The Truth: While there are many medications designed especially for PMS, other methods also reduce or eliminate symptoms. These include exercise, a low-fat and low-salt diet, and deep-relaxation techniques (see chapter 12). Your doctor can recommend a program designed especially for you.

Myth #3: *After your period begins, all PMS symptoms disappear.*

The Truth: While many symptoms are eliminated with the onset of menses, the term *pre*-menstrual is

WHY DO BOYS JOKE ABOUT PMS?

Sometimes, people poke fun at females' bad moods by accusing them of "being on the rag." This is a crude way of saying someone is suffering from PMS. While it may seem stupid or even cute to hear PMS jokes, this type of humor is anything but funny! Some people feel that females can't be trusted with important jobs or political offices (like President of the United States) because she might make a mistake or an irrational decision during PMS. You may help reduce this prejudice by speaking up the next time you hear someone sarcastically say, "she must be having PMS."

actually misleading. Many females suffer symptoms, such as soreness, fatigue, bloating, or irritability, for one or two days after their period starts. PMS symptoms can also occur fourteen or more days before a female's period begins. Any symptom related to your menstrual cycle—regardless of when it actually occurs—is called "premenstrual."

Body Self-Consciousness

Your body hasn't just been changing on the inside; your outsides are also being influenced by increased hormone levels. Your breasts are enlarging and your hips becoming rounder as you prepare for womanhood and possible childbearing.

No doubt you've noticed, and maybe even welcomed, these changes in your body. And you may also know that boys are noticing your changing shape, as well! You're likely becoming the object of some new-found attention from guys. Many girls are startled the first time someone whistles at her. She wonders, **"Are they whistling at me?"** Then she worries, **"Is this a compliment or an insult?"** Intuitively, though, most girls soon can tell the difference between an innocent whistle that says, "I think you're pretty," and a wolf whistle that says, "I'm thinking dirty thoughts about you."

If a guy says a suggestive or crude comment about your looks, the best retort is usually to ignore him. After all, these sort of folks thrive upon attention of any kind. If you yell at them, stick out your tongue at them, or anything similar, you're giving them what they want: your attention.

Sleeping Beauty: It Counts!

The quantity of sleep needed varies from person to person. The general rule is about eight to ten hours each night. How much sleep you get affects your ability to concentrate, your grades, your energy level, your sense of humor, how you get along with other people, and even your appetite! In fact, sleep affects our mental and physical health so much that medical researchers and hospital facilities specialize in the study of sleep. Here are some of their findings on how you can get a better night's sleep:

• **Make sure your bed and bedroom are comfortable.** If you've outgrown your childhood bed, be sure to alert your parents to this fact. You need to have a bed you can stretch out on! Keep clean sheets on your bed, and maintain a cool, quiet, and dark bedroom; lights, noise, and excessive temperatures interfere with sleep.

• **Keep a consistent bedtime.** This helps your body establish and maintain a sleeping and waking rhythm. Try to keep the same bedtime hours, even on weekends.

• **Avoid stimulating substances or activities within three hours of bedtime.** As we fall asleep, our body temperature cools slightly, and our heart rate decreases. Late-night exercise interferes with sleep because it keeps the body's temperature elevated. Stimulants such as the caffeine in colas or chocolate keep the heart pumping at the wide-awake rate, as well.

- **Try to avoid the "falling asleep in front of the television" habit.** As you've probably discovered, it's harder to fall back to sleep once you get up and go into your bedroom.

Tell your parents, school nurse, or family physician of any sudden changes in your sleeping habits. Chronic insomnia or sleeplessness are often symptoms of underlying physical or emotional problems that may require professional help.

JUST CAN'T SLEEP?

On nights when you can't fall asleep, try these tried-and-true tips to get those eyes shut:

❤ Drink hot chamomile decaffeinated herbal tea with some milk in it. Chamomile and warm milk have soothing effects on the body, helping it to sleep.

❤ Read something boring or pretend that you are forced to stay awake. Yes, sometimes you can trick yourself into falling asleep!

❤ Slowly stretch each muscle in your body. Have you ever seen a cat stretch in this way? That's a good way to relax uptight muscle groups, and let go of tension, which may be keeping you awake.

❤ Write down anything that's bugging you if you're afraid you'll forget to do it tomorrow.

Exercise and Emotions

As we discussed at the beginning of this book, scientists and psychologists often disagree about the nature and origin of

Exercise helps to elevate and balance moods.

emotions. Practically one of their only areas of agreement is this: *Exercise helps to elevate and balance moods.*

Studies conducted at universities and medical centers around the globe conclude that moderate and consistent exercise is more effective than any other method at lowering both stress and depression. The key words are moderate and consistent, however. Infrequent or inconsistent exercise (less than three times a week), or too-frequent exercise (see "Exercise Addictions" following) will not give you positive emotional benefits.

Exercise triggers production of a brain chemical called "**serotonin**." This chemical greatly influences mood, energy level, and appetite. Serotonin is created daily, and if your levels are too low, you feel cranky, sluggish, and excessively hungry. Poor lifestyle habits, including stress, insomnia, and imbalanced diets, also lower serotonin levels. Since exercise stimulates production of serotonin, a workout is one of the best ways to conquer fatigue or irritability.

EXERCISE ADDICTIONS

Can too much of a good thing be harmful? With exercise, the answer is "yes." Sometimes people become hooked on exercise and—like any other addiction—it causes problems in their lives. If you or someone you know seems to have two or more of these symptoms below, she may exercise too much. Symptoms of exercise addiction:

➤ **Insists on exercising** once, twice, or even three times nearly every day.

➤ **Refuses to skip an exercise session,** even when ill or injured.

➤ The amount of time spent exercising is causing **problems with friendships,** family relationships, or school.

➤ Has experienced more than one **injury** from exercising.

➤ Is **irritable or depressed** much of the time.

➤ Has a very **low body weight** or body fat percentage.

Like other compulsive behaviors, exercise addiction creates lifestyle problems. For one thing, if all your spare time is invested in working up a sweat, you won't be able to maintain your grades or friendships. Some exercise addicts feel unable to slow down their fitness program, even when they've injured a muscle. This can lead to permanent muscular damage.

THE GREAT OUTDOORS

"Go play outside!" *Who hasn't heard this strong suggestion from Mom or Dad?* Yet, spending time outdoors is more than a way to get you out of the house. There are many emotional and physical benefits for you, too.

Studies show that sunshine stimulates the production of the brain chemical, serotonin (mentioned earlier), which is why you may feel better on a sunny afternoon than on an overcast or rainy day. Of course, regardless of how you spend your time outside, you'll want to protect your skin with a lotion containing at least a fifteen sun protection factor (SPF) level.

Feelings and Physical Health

Here's a final and very important point about the connection between the body and emotions. **many physical problems** *are caused by* **unexpressed feelings.** People who hold in anger, or who don't get help for depression or anxiety, are prone to physical problems such as headaches, stomachaches, irregular heart rhythms, and back pain.

Your physical health is just one more good reason to get to know your emotions. The more you understand yourself, the easier it will be to express your feelings in appropriate ways.

You **CAN Deal With It!**

It's inevitable. If your body hasn't started its development toward womanhood, it will soon. But you know what? You're not alone! So, when you start feeling like you are the only person in the world to experience those changes, talk to a friend, aunt, cousin, or even, yes, your mom! You'll be amazed at how understanding they'll be.

CHAPTER 5

Eating and Emotions

I have this friend who has anorexia. She looks terrible! But the sad thing is that she acts so weird about everything, nobody wants to be around her.

—Tannis Gail, age 13, Ft. Collins, Colorado

Many girls become concerned about their weight around the time of adolescence. High-fashion magazines and other kids at school tell you that a pretty figure is an important asset in popularity.

But sometimes this concern seriously erodes the self-esteem or becomes an all-consuming obsession. The girl skips meals, takes laxatives, or over-exercises to lose weight. She checks her body weight and measurements throughout the day. And most of her thoughts and behavior center around how much she weighs. At that point, her behavior is no longer normal. She has an eating disorder.

Eating Disorders

Some girls become so preoccupied with every pound on their bathroom scale and every little fat gram or calorie they eat, that they become obsessed. This is the beginning of an eating disorder.

Eating disorders are a form of addictive behavior. In the beginning, the behavior is done with a conscious decision. For example, the girl will tell herself that she'll skip lunch in order to lose weight. But over time, the behavior becomes more and more habitual until she feels as if she has no choice. At that point, the girl may feel afraid or unable to eat any lunch. Or, she may binge on huge amounts of junk food, then force herself to vomit in order to "undo" the food consumption. She feels self-disgust after the act, and swears never to do it again. But a few hours later, she repeats the binge-purge cycle all over again.

ANOREXIA NERVOSA

The ultra-skinny, boyish figure, known as the "waif look," has come in and out of vogue throughout recorded history. However, the desire to have a supermodel's figure can go awry, and grow into the eating disorder known as **anorexia nervosa** or anorexia for short.

Girls with anorexia literally starve and over-exercise their bodies in order to achieve smaller and smaller weights and body sizes. Most people with anorexia say they "feel fat" even when their bodies are at extremely low weights. They point to

a minutely small bulge in their stom-
achs, hips, or thighs as evidence of
their "obesity." This confusion is called
distorted body image. In other
words, the girl really does believe she's
fat! It's as if her eyes deceive her when
she looks at her body in the mirror.

This preoccupation with weight and
clothing size is actually a symptom of serious
emotional problems. People with anorexia often feel their
weight, eating, and exercise are the only things they can control in their lives. Through their own efforts, they can gain or
lose the weight they want.

> **This preoccupation with weight
> and clothing size**
> *is actually a symptom of serious
> emotional problems.*

For some, anorexia is a form of suicidal behavior. A girl
may try to starve herself to death, either because she feels
unworthy of being alive or as a way to gain revenge upon parents whom she perceives as being unloving or abusive.
Unfortunately, her dieting efforts go too far and she may
become addicted to the feelings of power and success she gets
from losing weight.

When the scale registers a drop in weight, the eating-disordered girl feels she has succeeded. When she gains weight,
she feels she has lost control and "failed." When people tell

her she's too thin, she assumes those people are lying or are jealous of her.

Anorexia will kill its victim if not properly treated. Some of its deadly side effects include:

Malnourishment. When the body is starved of necessary nutrients, it's not a pretty picture. Far from looking svelte and glamorous, malnourished people are **susceptible to illness, have low energy, and dull, lifeless skin, eyes, hair, and fingernails.** They are prone to fainting spells, which could cause serious accidents. Their concentration and memory are severely impaired, resulting in problems at school, work, and in social settings.

Electrolyte imbalances. **Electrolytes** are the electrical-like charges that operate the brain and basic body functions. These charges are dependent upon a proper balance of potassium, sodium, and magnesium in the body. People who starve themselves or who purge by forced vomiting or laxative abuse, usually deplete their electrolyte balance. Many eating-disordered people **die sudden deaths** due to electrical short-circuiting in the brain and/or heart caused by electrolyte imbalances.

Dehydration. The anorexic girl may avoid drinking fluids because of mistaken beliefs that they make her body heavier, or make her retain water. This practice is **deadly** if it leads the body to become dangerously dehydrated.

Unattractive appearance. Malnourishment and dehydration from anorexia leave the body more vulnerable to viruses, bacteria, and even cold weather. Such vulnerability triggers the face and body to grow excessive hair as it attempts to ward away cold air. So it's common for anorexic girls to have **a lot of peach fuzz on their faces.**

Often, an anorexic feels **depressed** from malnourishment and low self-esteem, and her facial expression and body posture reflect this. (By the way, many anorexics seek treatment solely to try to fix their devastating appearance, rather than because of any of the other health risks associated with self-starvation.)

These are just some of the negative and deadly side effects of anorexia. Treatment for anorexia is challenging, because the doctor is asking the girl to do something that she considers a sign of failure: to eat and gain some weight. It's an illness that many young women battle for the rest of their lives.

BULIMIA NERVOSA

Bulimia nervosa, often called bulimia, is another eating disorder. The term "bulimia" means

> ### DO YOU KNOW SOMEONE WHO'S EATING DISORDERED?
>
> Maybe you know a girl at school who throws up her lunch every day. Did you know that she's probably suffering from bulimia? Symptoms of anorexia include secrecy about eating or dieting, shopping or cooking a lot for others, and excessive exercise. If you suspect that one of your friends or acquaintances may have an eating problem, you could save a life by talking to her, or reporting it (anonymously, if you like) to a school counselor.

"appetite of an ox," and no wonder! Bulimia involves **binge-eating** huge amounts of food, usually easy-to-swallow, high-calorie foods such as ice cream, dough-nuts, or cookie dough.

After the girl's stomach is full, she takes steps to eliminate the calories to avoid weight gain. This is called "**purging**." The most common purging methods are sticking one's finger down one's throat to induce vomiting, taking a laxative, or excessive exercising.

Bulimia is dangerous because, like the self-starvation behavior of anorexia, purging rids the brain and body of vital electrolytes—the chemical messengers that keep the body running. **Many girls with bulimia die suddenly** because their electrolyte levels became perilously low, and their hearts or brains stopped operating. Other bulimia-related deaths occur from suicide (purging can increase depression) or choking on vomit.

Bulimics are sometimes overweight because they consume enormous quantities of high-calorie, high-fat foods during an eating binge. Purging isn't just dangerous; it's also a *very ineffective* way to lose weight. It's virtually impossible to rid one's self of all the food consumed during a binge, even through the extreme measures tried by bulimics.

Girls who force themselves to vomit develop **chipmunk-like pouches in their cheeks. Their teeth are usually brown and filled with cavities,** as their vomit's gastric acid erodes tooth enamel. In fact, many dentists are the first to detect bulimia in their patients by recognizing this key symptom.

> # Q: DO BOYS BECOME EATING DISORDERED?
>
> **A:** Mainly girls suffer from eating disorders. Boys only comprise ten percent of patients treated for eating disorders. Usually, boys with eating disorders are in a sport or profession that demands a low body weight such as wrestling, horse racing, or modeling. Boys with eating disorders express a great deal of shame for having a "female problem," which is one reason why males put off seeking treatment until their body weight becomes dangerously low.

What You Eat Makes a Difference

The foods you eat and liquids you consume also affect your emotions. You've probably felt tired after eating Thanksgiving dinner. Two reasons why this happens: first, the sheer amount of food consumed can make you feel sluggish! Second, turkey contains an **amino acid** (protein building block) called "L-Tryptophan," which creates brain chemicals that make you feel sleepy. Chicken, dairy products, and bananas also contain high amounts of L-Tryptophan.

Many foods and beverages have amino acids and other properties that alter moods or energy levels:

Stimulants (Increases blood pressure and/or heart rate)

❁ Caffeine in coffee, tea, colas, and chocolate

❁ Tyramine and tyrosine in aged cheese and pickled foods

- ✿ MSG (monosodium glutamate, the preservative used in some Oriental restaurants)

- ✿ Sweeteners, such as sugar and Aspartame (an artificial sweetener used in diet products)

Calming foods (Produces brain chemicals that make you feel relaxed or sleepy)

- ✿ Carbohydrates (breads, pasta, rice, grains)

- ✿ Dairy products (contains L-Tryptophan)

- ✿ Turkey and chicken (also contains L-Tryptophan)

Food Cravings and Emotions

Sometimes people think they're hungry for food, when in reality, they're experiencing an uncomfortable emotion such as sadness, anger, or boredom. Instead of facing the feeling, they decide to eat in order to **block** awareness of the emotion. This is called "emotional eating," meaning that the hunger is based in emotions and not in true physical hunger.

For example, when twelve-year-old Tracy's parents announced they were divorcing, the Dallas preteen felt sad and upset. Tracy also wondered if she were partly to blame. She noticed that whenever she ate food, she felt a little better. When Tracy ate ice cream, doughnuts, or cookies, she'd temporarily forget about her parent's divorce. A month after her father moved out of the family home, Tracy gained ten pounds.

We've probably all engaged in emotional eating at one time or another. Usually, it's not a problem unless it creates a significant, unwanted weight gain, as in Tracy's case, or if it leads to a habit of eating junk food.

Two ways to combat emotional eating are:

1. Learn to tell the difference between emotional and physical hunger.

2. Stay away from food for fifteen minutes whenever emotional hunger occurs.

Emotional and physical hunger feel identical, until you tune into these key differences:

- Emotional hunger is *sudden* (one minute you're fine, the next moment you think you're starving), while physical hunger is gradual and occurs over a period of time.

- Emotional hunger is experienced *in your head and mouth,* while physical hunger occurs in your stomach.

- Emotional hunger is usually for a *specific food* ("I must eat pepperoni pizza—no other food will do!"), while physical hunger is open to other food choices.

- Emotional hunger creates *urgent feelings* that you must eat immediately (in order to block awareness of painful emotions), while physical hunger is calmer and creates a desire to eat sometime in the near future.

So, the next time you get a craving for chocolate cake after a really stressful day at school, check it out and see if you could be experiencing emotional hunger instead of true physical hunger. If it is a food craving based in emotion, ask yourself this question, "What feeling am I trying to block out with food?" Usually, the first answer that pops into your head is correct. (On the other hand, sometimes it is okay to give in and eat some chocolate cake!)

You CAN Deal With It!

One of the most effective ways to stay happy and healthy is to eat right. Keep track of everything you eat and when you eat for a week. Include the handful of M&M's you grabbed out of the candy dish, as well as the two helpings of broccoli you put away at dinner (yeah, sure). Are you getting enough fruits and vegetables? Do you notice that you ate when you weren't hungry? The best way to avoid eating problems in the future is to form healthy eating habits today!

CHAPTER 6

Happy Days

I guess I'm pretty happy most of the time. I just wish I didn't have so much homework and chores to do! That's the only thing that makes me unhappy. Plus, my little brother bugs me a lot. But most things are pretty good.

— Tracy Cook, age 12, Lincolnshire, Illinois

What makes you happy? Wearing a new outfit? Receiving a birthday present? **Going somewhere with your best friend?** Probably the things that make you happy today are different from the things you enjoyed as a little girl.

As you read earlier, your thoughts have a lot of influence over the emotions you feel. This is good news, because it means that by changing the contents of your thoughts, you can actually boost your self-esteem, confidence, and mood!

Let's say you're in the middle of a crisis. Would you solve the problem more effectively if you had a clear, cool head or if you were totally upset? Of course, a cool-headed you is more likely to come up with a creative solution. That's why it's so important to stop in the middle of any crisis, take a breath, and if possible, walk away from the situation for a moment. When your thoughts and emotions settle a bit, you're less apt to say or do something regrettable. Plus, you may come up with a solution or more positive perspective about the situation!

Happiness is one of the most basic of all human emotions, and people are naturally built to be happy. When negative emotions are cleared away, what's left is our true and natural state of feeling confident and good about ourselves. Having high self-esteem and pleasant moods may be easier to attain and maintain than you imagine.

Instant Mood Builders

Here are some simple, yet powerful methods to beat a bad mood in a hurry:

1. ***Decide to be happy.*** It's not fun to be in a bad mood, is it? When you find yourself thinking depressing thoughts such as, "No one understands me!" instead, decide to think, "There are many things about me that are great. I am sweet, smart, and caring. I deserve to be happy, and I give myself permission to feel good right now." These positive thoughts are called **affirmations**. Keep concentrating on the affirmations, and watch your mood shift to a more pleasant state. You'll be amazed at the power your thoughts have over your emotions!

2. ***Think about someone or something that makes you happy.*** Thinking of your pet cat, a flower garden, or a favorite dessert, may all help you smile. Whatever it is, allow yourself to escape into a peaceful moment of enjoyment. You can feel even better by transferring those good feelings to other areas of your life.

Here's how: Think about a fun activity with your friends, for example. Let this imagined scene fill you with excitement. Your mood will reflect a contagious level of happiness, and you'll find that other people are drawn to you, attracted by your enthusiasm and warmth.

3. ***Surprise someone.*** Everyone loves to receive a gift or kind gesture. And it's so much fun to be the person who thinks up a pleasant surprise. Allow your imagination to run wild, and you'll come up with dozens of little ways to surprise your family and friends. For example, do a much-needed errand for your mother without being asked. Or give your best friend a magazine that has an article about her favorite movie star. Bake your dad's favorite cake. You'll quickly find the truth of the phrase, "It's better to give than to receive."

4. ***Write a gratitude list.*** Here's a method guaranteed to turn a frown into a smile in a big hurry! Make yourself write a list of everything for which you are grateful. Start out with the obvious, such as "I'm grateful that I have a

bicycle, I'm in good health, I have a home to live in, and so on." Keep going and think of more specific things and people for whom you are grateful. Think about all the people you know and live with. Think about how, even though there are moments of disagreements, these people bring love and learning into your life. The more you realize how lucky you are, the more thankful—and happy—you'll feel.

5. **Enjoy something humorous.** Laughter truly is medicine for the heart. Watch a funny movie, read a funny book, call a good-humored friend, or open the daily newspaper to the comics page.

One good laugh can chase away hours of sorrow!

6. **Call or write an old friend.** This is an instant mood-booster! You can pour your heart out to someone who knows and shares your life history. This will make you feel closer to your friend, as well as help you get your problems off your chest.

7. **Complete something you've been procrastinating on.** Have you been putting off some unpleasant, yet necessary task? Something such as a history project, writing a thank-you note, or cleaning out your closet? Believe it or not, these are good things to do to chase away the blues. The reason: After you accomplish a much-needed task, there's a big feeling of relief. You'll thank yourself for getting the whole thing over with!

8. ***Do something physical.*** You know the Nike shoe commercial that says, "Just do it"? Well, that advice applies perfectly anytime you wish to snap out of a lousy mood. Studies show that a person who is depressed often isolates herself (or himself) in her home or bedroom. She

stays in a bad mood partly because she acts in depressing ways: staying in her room, not getting dressed, and sleeping a lot. To break this cycle, psychologists advise pushing the depressed person to get up, get dressed, and get out of the house.

If you find yourself sleeping a lot or just hanging in your room doing nothing, here are some suggestions to help you get physical!

* Take your dog (or your neighbor's dog) for a brisk walk.

* Go to the park and play on the swings, slides, and jungle gym—you're never to old to play.

* Rake the leaves, mow the lawn, or shovel the walk—whatever is season-appropriate!

* If weather is poor, pop an exercise video into the VCR and sweat to your favorite video instructor.

HAPPINESS IS A CHOICE

Happiness is one of the most pleasant and preferred of all the different emotions. It's also an emotion over which we have much power and control.

. . . if we all <u>enjoy</u> feeling happy, and we all have the <u>power</u> to feel happy, how come we're not happier more often?

So, if we all *enjoy* feeling happy, and we all have the *power* to feel happy, how come we're not happier more often? The reasons vary, but most unhappiness is a result of a "block"—a thought or belief that interferes with being happy. These blocks cause people to deny themselves opportunities for happiness.

Blocks are very common and normal. Psychologists teach their clients how to identify and remove these blocks. This self-knowledge enables people to live a happier and more fulfilling life.

Here are a few of the more common blocks to happiness:

Suspiciousness or fears about happiness. This is the belief that punishment, emotional pain, or simply something bad will follow good, such as, "This happiness won't last for long, so I better not allow myself to get used to it!"

Guilt or undeservingness. These painful emotions come from believing you don't deserve good experiences to happen to you. Someone harboring guilt believes, "Other people deserve happiness, but I'm not good enough to get what I want."

Procrastinating on happiness. Some people focus only on the future instead of enjoying the present moment. They often put conditions on happiness, such as, "I won't be happy until I'm old enough to drive."

Unhealthy habits. Happiness is also blocked by unhealthy lifestyle habits that leave the body feeling tired and sluggish.

Some people mistakenly believe they will be happier or raise their mood by eating junk food, using drugs or alcohol, skipping exercise, or staying up all night—crazy! **When it comes to bad habits, JUST SAY NO!**

Unfinished grief. When we experience a major loss or change, such as the death of a loved one, parental divorce, or a household move, grief is a natural reaction. Grief usually subsides within a few months, unless it is held in or repressed. Holding in sadness or anger about a loss is a major block to happiness. Some people need professional counseling to overcome their grief.

Worries. Everyone worries occasionally, but for some people, it's a negative habit that interferes with happiness. Many worries involve obsessing about "**what if something bad happens to me.**" One good method for dealing with these worrisome thoughts is to write them down. When you see your worries written in ink, you often realize how unlikely it is that your fears would ever come true. You also might realize some actions you could take to prevent your worst fears from becoming a reality.

Thinking depressing thoughts. Anyone can talk themselves into a bad mood by telling themselves a downer thought such as, "I'm not pretty," or "No one likes me." If you catch yourself having negative thoughts, silently tell yourself to "Stop!" Then immediately think an affirming thought like, "I have the thickest hair in my family. I love my hair!" or "I have two really special friends." It may take awhile, but stick with it. Eventually you'll feel better.

If You're Happy and You Know It . . .

No one expects you to be in a great mood one hundred percent of the time. Still, you've now learned some ways to direct your emotions to feeling brighter and more cheery.

As you become more aware of your changing feelings, you'll also have a greater understanding of your personal emotional patterns. You'll understand what kind of situations make you feel the best, as well as the types of circumstances that tend to frustrate you. Getting to know yourself is an important part of growing older.

You CAN Deal With It!

• • • • • • • • • • • • • • • • • • • •

Have you made your gratitude list, as described on pages 55 and 56? If not, do it today. Get a piece of poster board and post it on your wall in your bedroom. Write everything you are thankful for on the poster. Keep a colorful marker close by to add to the gratitude list whenever you feel like it.

CHAPTER 7

It's a Bummer!

> Last week, my dog Alfie got hit by a car. I can't stop thinking about him, and at night I cry a lot. My mom says we can get a new dog, but it wouldn't be the same. I miss Alfie so much!
>
> — Kimberly Louradian, age 10, Stamford, Connecticut

You're bound to feel down or depressed once in a while. Maybe you receive some bad news, or perhaps a friend hurts your feelings.

Whatever the cause, understanding *what* emotion you're feeling will help you to feel better. Even though the situation might still be a bummer, you'll feel some relief just by knowing what your exact emotions are.

Tangled Emotions

Sometimes, you experience a mixture of feelings. For example, let's say you find out that a girl at school whom you don't really like is having a birthday party, and you're not invited. You might feel a combination of emotions: relief (because you honestly don't enjoy her company), envy (because some of your friends are invited to the party), and frustration (because you don't want to be upset over the situation). These are normal reactions that most girls would experience under similar circumstances!

Mixed emotions can be confusing, and even upsetting, because you're trying to respond to several feelings at once, rather than dealing with one emotion. One way to diffuse their intensity is through understanding what different emotions you are experiencing, and *why* you feel each of them.

FEELINGS CHECKLIST

Here's a list of some emotions you may feel. Whenever you're confused about your feelings, consult this list and note which emotions seem to fit. On a separate piece of paper, write down all the emotions that apply to you right now. Being honest with yourself is the first step toward feeling better.

Afraid Confused *Grateful* Lighthearted

SCARED Aggravated *Curious* D E P R E S S E D

GENEROUS Lively Shy

AMUSED *Deceived* Glad *Loving*

Silly ANGRY Delighted Good

Merry Stressed Annoyed guilty

Mischievous Successful Appreciative
Disappointed happy
Misunderstood Sunny ASHAMED
Embarrassed Hopeful Nervous Thrilled
bashful Envious Inspired optimistic
TRIUMPHANT Bothered Excited!
INTERESTED Pleased upset Cheerful
EXHILARATED IRRITATED PRESSURED Victorious
bored IMPATIENT
CLUMSY Fascinated Jealous C Relaxed
Vibrant Confident O Free
JOLLY Relieved WANTED O
FURIOUS JOYFUL Sad L Worried

Understanding Your Emotions

Let's take a closer look at some of the more "troublesome" feelings you're likely to encounter.

Disappointment

You were counting on getting a bicycle for Christmas . . . and you didn't. You really wanted to go with your best friend's family to that amusement park . . . and you couldn't. You thought you'd get a Valentine's card from that guy you have a crush on . . . and it didn't happen.

Life is filled with letdowns, and the natural emotional

companion is disappointment. Luckily, there are many ways to deal with disappointment:

→ Try to **find a bright side** or a learned lesson from the situation. Remember that disappointments help us to learn patience and perseverance, and strengthen us for future challenges in life.

✳ Channel your disappointment by **polishing your skills** to improve your chances for success the next time. If you tried out for the cheerleading squad and didn't make it, find out why. Do you need to spend extra time practicing your jumps? Should you find someone who can help you perfect your tumbling skills?

→ If someone disappointed you, **be honest** with him or her about your feelings—in a nice way! By making the other person aware of how his or her behavior affected you, you may avoid future disappointment by inspiring the other person to be more thoughtful next time.

✳ **Talk with a trusted friend.** It feels good to be heard and understood, and your friend may point out a different or more positive way of looking at the situation.

→ Write about your feelings in a journal. **List the reasons** you are disappointed, and write at least one thing that is positive about the present situation, such as, "Since I didn't make the drill team, I'll have more time to be with friends."

Jealousy and Envy

It seems like some kids have it made, doesn't it? They've got nicer clothes, a cuter boyfriend, or better grades than you, and you don't like it! The emotion you may feel varies from jealousy to envy. Here's how to tell apart these two distinctly different emotions.

Jealousy is when you feel threatened with losing something or someone valuable to you. For example, you may feel jealous when your boyfriend talks to another girl if you fear he will like her more than you.

Envy is when you feel emotional pain because you desire to have what somebody else has. You may feel envious, for instance, because you wanted to be captain of the soccer team and someone else was chosen. However, with envy, you may want something someone else has, but you don't necessarily want to keep that person from having it. While in jealousy, you don't want to share it with anyone!

Of the two, jealousy is a more difficult emotion to deal with because it makes you feel helpless or out of control. Jealousy stems from feeling angry and afraid that you could lose someone or something you value.

Envy, on the other hand, can actually inspire you to improve your life. Let's say you envy a girl at school who always gets A's. You can use the energy of your envy in a positive way by studying longer and harder.

Worry

Do you ever have thoughts about the future that scare or depress you? If so, you have probably been worrying. Worry is a way of trying to predict what might happen so that you can prepare for it or even intervene and make things better.

Unfortunately, worry usually does nothing to fix the future, and it also wrecks the present moment you're in!

> **The best way to deal with worry is to write down everything that you're thinking about. Put a star next to those things you can control and put a line through those things you can't . . .**

Your list will immediately look more manageable! Now, next to each starred item, jot down an idea or two of what you can do to fix the situation. Then do it! (*But,* don't worry about how you'll get everything done—just take it one day at a time!)

Boredom

"I'm bored!"

How many times have you sat in your room, feeling as if there was absolutely nothing fun or interesting to do?

Boredom can be a source of stress. Many kids and adults allow boredom to dampen their zest for life. Take steps now to learn how to conquer boredom with these boredom busters:

Start a business. Baby-sitting, car washing, dog walking,

 errand running, gardening, house-sitting, pet-sitting, or writing and printing a neighborhood newsletter are just a few business ideas to chase boredom away.

Join a club. Check out the clubs offered through your school, church or temple, Girl Scouts, YWCA or YMCA, or community recreation center. You'll have fun, meet new people, and maybe learn a new hobby, language, or sport. Or, start your own club with some friends!

Start a collection. Collect anything that interests you, such as stamps, baseball or other sports trading cards, rare coins, stickers, or glass animals.

Join a sports team. This is guaranteed to keep you fit and busy! Your school, local gym, or recreation center offers many options for year-round team sports.

Volunteer to do some fun work. If you love animals, maybe an animal shelter could use your services. A plant nursery, nursing home, hospital, or a day care center are a few other places that could use you!

Make one new friend a week. Every friend you'll ever have is, in the beginning, a stranger. Make a point to say "Hi" and start a conversation with one kid at school each week, and you'll rapidly make many new friends who will keep you busy.

Write to a pen pal. Your teacher or favorite magazine are good resources for finding pen pals all over the world. It's interesting to correspond with people in different countries and learn about their lives and experiences.

Guilt

When you feel bad because you've made a mistake or done something wrong (whether intentionally or not), your conscience creates the painful emotion known as guilt. Most of the time, guilt helps to keep us in line; that is, we try to behave in right and honest ways in order to avoid feeling this painful emotion.

The best way to avoid guilt, then, is to do your best to obey rules at home and school. But if you do make a mistake or occasionally forget about a rule, don't be too hard on your-self. Apologize, fix, or clean up your error, and then vow to try to never repeat the mistake. Learning from our errors is one way in which we grow into maturity. After all, nobody's born knowing everything!

Sometimes, though, feelings of guilt become overwhelming and consuming. Some people have feelings of guilt that have nothing to do with accidentally spilling milk at the dinner table. These people feel guilty all the time, as if there is some-thing wrong with them as human beings. Very often, people abused in childhood grow up thinking they are "bad people" who deserve to be punished. Usually, these intense feelings of guilt require professional help.

Impatience

> "I can't <u>wait</u> to get my driver's license!"
> *How much longer until my birthday?*
> "**When** are we getting to Grandma's house?"

Sometimes it seems as if the good stuff in life takes a zillion years to happen. It's tough to wait when you're really looking forward to getting a present or a new privilege.

Impatience is a feeling of wanting the future to be here—now. It's a combination of excite-ment, anticipation, and frustration—defi-nitely not a pleasant emotion to have for very long!

Here's one way to eliminate impa-tience:

1. First, recall a time when something exciting was about to happen (such as a special holiday).

2. Remember how hyped you were just thinking about the events of the day. Allow yourself to recapture those pleasant feelings of anticipation.

3. Realize that the anticipation and looking forward to that special event was half the fun!

Often, our expectations are more pleasant than the actual activity. So, the next time you're looking forward to something, allow yourself to enjoy the sweet feeling of anticipation.

INSTEAD OF GETTING ALL CAUGHT UP IN FRUSTRATING THOUGHTS, **CONCENTRATE ON THE PLEASANT BUTTERFLIES IN YOUR STOMACH.**

Some impatience is caused by a desire to grow up in a hurry. You dream of the day when you'll have more freedom, your own money, and an adult lifestyle. But slow down, girl! While adulthood definitely has advantages, it also has its share of pressures (like bills, work, and taking care of a family). Why not savor these remaining years when your parents are supporting you, so that you'll truly have pleasant memories of your youth?

Sadness

Everyone experiences occasional blue moods. Any number of things can trigger sadness: an upsetting movie, losing a pet, being grounded, or having a friend move to a different city.

Sometimes, sadness seems to occur for no reason at all. You just feel down, and you don't know why! This is perfectly normal, and as long as the sad mood is gone within a day or two, it's nothing to worry about.

The Serious Side of Emotions

Sometimes, emotions can seem overwhelming. No matter how much your friends try to cheer you up, all you can do is cry. Just like a cold can run the gamut from sniffles to life-threatening pneumonia, emotions can also have extreme ranges.

DEPRESSION

Have you ever felt like you wanted to stay under the covers all day long? *So sad, you didn't want to see or talk to anyone?* Those feelings are a small sample of what depression is like.

Studies indicate that self-esteem levels play a big part in determining whether someone becomes depressed or not. People most at risk for depression include those with *variable* self-esteem—that is, feeling good about themselves one day, and disliking themselves the next—*especially when self-esteem hinges upon external circumstances.*

For example, if a girl's self-esteem is dependent on the number of compliments she receives, she would be prone to depression on days when others didn't compliment her. In contrast, a girl who merely enjoys receiving compliments, but whose self-esteem stays steady no matter how many compliments she does or doesn't receive, would be less prone to depression. The first girl's self-image is completely controlled by others' behavior, while the second girl's self-image is less dependent on others' behavior. With practice, anyone can develop the healthier habits of the second girl, improving self-esteem and lessening chances of depression.

Depression that lasts longer than a day or two can turn into a serious psychological problem. Most people who try to commit suicide suffer from depression, so doctors are very careful to properly diagnose this mood disorder.

Treatment for depression ranges from meeting with a therapist on a regular basis to taking anti-depressant medications. In extreme cases, usually when the threat of suicide exists, depressed people are hospitalized.

Females are twice as likely to be treated for depression, as compared to males. This doesn't necessarily mean that gals are more depressed than guys, just that females seek help for depression at twice the rate as males.

Also, depression seems to run in families. A depressed person is almost three times more likely than a non-depressed person to have a close family member who has suffered from clinical depression. Whether this is genetic or a learned way of living is still undecided.

TEENS WHO TAKE THEIR OWN LIVES

Sometimes sad emotions lead to very serious consequences.

No doubt you've heard about the percentage of teenage deaths that happen by suicide. Maybe you even know someone who took their own life. Suicide is the second leading cause of death among Americans aged fifteen to twenty-four. The number of teens who commit suicide has increased dramatically—150 percent!—compared to twenty years ago. Government studies say that

> The number of teens who commit suicide has increased dramatically—**150%**—compared to twenty years ago.

thirty-three percent of all eighth through tenth graders have given thought to suicide.

Suicide is a permanent solution to a temporary problem. Many teens mistakenly believe that life isn't worth living, that no one cares about them, and that nothing will ever improve. Some teenagers take their own lives after experimenting with drugs or alcohol. Then there are teens who kill themselves to take revenge upon a parent or boyfriend/girlfriend who they see as unloving. Other suicides happen as a result of involvement with cults.

It goes without saying that all attempts at suicide have tragic consequences. Teens who try suicide, but survive, are usually hospitalized in a psychiatric ward. Sometimes, their self-inflicted wounds create horrible physical problems that last a lifetime, such as paralysis, loss of a limb or eyesight, and scars or facial disfigurement.

So what can you do to help curtail this tragic epidemic? For one thing, you can be alert to signals that a friend or acquaintance may be on the edge of a suicide attempt. While not every suicidal person drops clues to his or her intentions, most do. After all, the person really doesn't want to die—he or she simply wants their intense emotional pain to stop. If you spot one or more of these signs, tell a school counselor, parent, or trusted teacher about your concerns right away. You may be able to help save someone's life!

Signs of Suicidal Tendencies

Here are the signs of a person who is contemplating taking his or her life. It's important to take these signs seriously, and seek appropriate help for the person in trouble.

➤ Makes **comments** such as, "I wish I were dead" or "I'd like to disappear forever." Take these words seriously! Ask the person if he or she is considering suicide. Contrary to myth, this doesn't "plant" the idea in a person's head; it gives him or her a chance to discuss intentions.

➤ A sudden and extreme **interest in guns, knives, sleeping pills, or other deadly methods**, as well as an obsession about other people who have taken their lives.

➤ **Giving away prized possessions** and getting their life into a final order.

➤ Extreme **sadness** and crying.

➤ Staying **isolated,** especially when this is not a normal pattern for the person.

➤ An intense **focus on depressing music** (with lyrics that glorify death or suicide), books, or illustrations. This can include items with references of death such as skulls, the grim reaper, pentagrams, or dark occult materials.

➤ Has had **five or more of the following symptoms** for at least fourteen straight days:
   - ✓ depressed mood
   - ✓ lack of interest in anything
   - ✓ weight gain or loss by at least five percent
   - ✓ sleeps a lot or not at all
   - ✓ seems to be in either fast or slow motion
   - ✓ is always tired
   - ✓ puts self down and/or feels guilty a lot
   - ✓ can't concentrate

Help Is Here!

No one is expected to be bright and cheery every minute of every day. We all have bad moods and bad days. But for some people, every day's a bad day! If you or anyone you care about exhibits the signs listed above, help is definitely advisable. There are a lot of people who are qualified to help.

School Counselors: This professional counselor works in your school office, and is there to help you emotionally, as well as academically. This person is often a good starting place for kids seeking help for dealing with depression, problems learning or concentrating, or family issues such as divorce, child abuse, or parental substance abuse. The school counselor can give comfort, advice, and referrals to **psychologists** or **psychiatrists** if necessary. And if you are concerned about a troubled friend, the school counselor is also a good person to turn to.

Hotlines and Helplines: If you need help in a hurry, or just want answers to some deeply personal concerns, hotlines are a good source of emotional support, information, and referrals to local helping professionals. Most hotlines have a toll-free number, and their services are confidential and free of charge. There's a list of several good hotlines in the back of this book. You can also find hotline listings in the front of your phone directory or by calling directory assistance. Your 911 operator can also help in times of dire emergency, such as a suicide threat or attempt.

Medical Doctors and Psychiatrists: These professionals have earned a medical degree, and they are licensed to prescribe medications for mental disorders. Usually, extreme cases of depression are treated by these professionals. However, your family doctor is a good person to talk to if you feel depressed or anxious for several weeks in a row. This doctor may prescribe helpful medication, or refer you to a psychiatrist for further evaluation and therapy.

Physicians and psychiatrists charge around one hundred dollars or more per visit. Your parents' medical insurance or public assistance healthcare may pay for these services.

Psychologists and Psychotherapists: These men and women hold a Ph.D. in psychology. They aren't medical doctors, so they can't prescribe drugs. However, they do have many techniques and methods designed to help alleviate depression. Some schools have psychologists on staff, and your school counselor or family physician can refer you to a reputable psychologist as well.

The services of a school psychologist are free, and your sessions together will involve you taking tests to determine your personality style, your emotional health, and your ability to process information. Psychologists and psychotherapists who aren't connected to your school may charge between fifty and one hundred dollars for each one-hour session. Some health insurance plans pay for these services.

Social Workers, Marriage and Family Counselors: These mental health workers hold Master's degrees in psychology or social work. They are highly qualified to help with personal and family issues, and they often have access to community resources to supplement their counseling services.

Costs range from forty to eighty dollars per session. Many social workers offer free or very low cost sessions through community mental health programs, which you can find by calling directory assistance or looking in the beginning of the yellow pages under your city's government section.

Clergy: The minister, rabbi, reverend, or priest of your church or synagogue can also provide helpful counseling, with a spiritual approach to treatment. Their services are usually free of charge; however, it is customary to give a nominal love donation of whatever money your family can afford.

You CAN
Deal With It!

Try another journaling experience, this time working with pictures instead of words. You may find relief from your strong emotions in drawing, painting, or coloring. Keep a journal full of your artwork depicting difficult emotions and how you dealt with them. For instance, if you were jealous of your sister's new trendy shoes, you could draw a picture of them. Then draw a picture of how you dealt with your emotions. Maybe you read a good book to keep your mind off the shoes, so draw a picture of a book. If you talked to your sister about it, you could draw both of you talking. Use your imagination!

$\mathcal{S}$tressed Out!

What drives me crazy is how my teachers give so much homework, and they all expect us to get everything done at the same time! I wish teachers would check with each other, so I wouldn't have three million book reports due and seven thousand tests to study for, all at the same time!

— Yolanda Lopez, age 13, Sierra Vista, Arizona

$\mathcal{H}$omework! Chores! After-school activities! Sometimes it seems like there aren't enough hours in the day to get everything done.

Time pressures are just one aspect of a condition called stress. Stress is an external condition that leads to an internal body state known as tension. **How do you know if you're stressed?** You will most likely have tightened muscles, shallow breathing, rapid pulse and heart rate, perspiration, and irritability. Stressful items, which lead to tension, are called "stressors."

Common stressors include: a **pop quiz** or final exam; a **fight** with a friend; pressure to **perform** well in sports, theater, or other activity; a **term paper** due the following day (which you haven't yet completed); or a major change in the **family structure** (job loss, financial problems, divorce, moving, new baby, or death).

There are two forms of stress:

Eustress (pronounced "you-stress"): Eustress is a pressure, concern, or activity that involves a positive event or change. For example, Christmas or Hanukkah may create eustress as you anxiously await opening gifts, feel excited to see a favorite relative, or hurriedly wrap the gift you made for your mom when she wasn't looking. Even though the holiday season is considered a positive event, it still creates a lot of stress.

Negative stress: This is a situation that no one would consider positive. You can probably think of a lot of examples of negative stress, such as a pop quiz, major homework assignments, and arguments with friends.

Are You Stressed Out?

Sometimes we're unaware that our moods and bodies are impacted by stress. We can't see the changes within us as clearly as can those around us. This checklist will help you determine if you're stressed out. Do any of these signs apply to you?

✗ People often complain that you are **moody, irritable, seem distracted, or stressed.**

✗ You frequently experience **pain in the back, neck, or shoulders** not connected to any accident.

✗ You often have **headaches** that occur for no reason.

✗ You tend to **grind your teeth,** or your **jaw frequently feels sore.**

✗ You have frequent **stomach upsets** unrelated to eating habits or illness.

✗ You experience a **major increase or decrease in your appetite.**

✗ Your **sleeping habits** have recently changed (insomnia, excessive sleepiness, bed-wetting, nightmares).

✗ You experience many of these simultaneously: **chronic worry, fear, anger, time concerns, irritability, or guilt.**

✗ **People keep telling you** to "relax" or "take it easy."

If you have three or more of the symptoms on the list, you are likely suffering from a poor reaction to life stress. As you read earlier, everyone reacts to life circumstances in his or her own way. For one person, an event like getting picked to act in a class play would be a major stressor, while someone else may consider it a pleasure!

Most people experience some kind of stress from time to time, *and usually stress is no big deal.*

In fact, it's really impossible to entirely escape stress. Plus, sometimes stress is a great motivator that pushes you to achieve your goals or improve yourself.

Stress and accompanying tension become a problem when it negatively affects your health or interferes with your happiness. Talk with a parent or your school nurse if you are having difficulty sleeping or are experiencing physical pain associated with stress. You don't have to needlessly suffer from stress, and you certainly needn't suffer alone!

Types of Stress and Some Solutions

Now that you've learned to identify whether or not you're experiencing symptoms of stress, the next step is to pinpoint the source of that stress. Here are some likely culprits:

BOREDOM

Believe it or not, boredom is stressful! Boredom means feeling unexcited or unchallenged. For example, these feelings can stem from being put in a beginner's class when your knowledge is already that of an intermediate or advanced student.

Lack of purpose or goals in one's life also creates boredom. Solutions include developing a new hobby, beginning a challenging project, or joining a cause to which you feel committed.

Monotony—doing the same thing, the same way, all the time—creates boredom, too. You can "shake up" your day a bit in small, simple ways such as talking to a new kid at school, rearranging your bedroom, or wearing a new hairstyle.

One of the reasons boredom is stressful is that it leaves unstructured time on your hands. Some people use that time to think depressing thoughts or worry about unimportant things. When you fill your time with interesting projects and friendships, you don't have as much time to fret.

IRRITANTS

Sometimes things and people just get on your nerves. These irritants are a common source of stress, but are one of the easiest to take care of. Here are examples and suggestions:

People: Irritating people are those adults and kids who rub you the wrong way. Sometimes, you just take an instant dislike to a person without really knowing why. Other times, you disapprove of someone's way of talking, joking around, acting, or even dressing. If someone consistently gets under your skin, you have a few choices.

1. Be honest. Saying something such as, "I really like you and want to be your friend, but I can't handle it when you act that way," is often all that's necessary. As long as you speak politely and respectfully, your words should be met with openness.

2. Write the person a brief note summarizing your feelings. Write your statements in ways that show you are taking responsibility for your feelings. For example, instead of writing "You make me mad when you . . . ," write "I feel angry when you . . ."

Can you spot the difference between these two statements? In the first, you are accusing the other person. His or her reaction will likely be defensiveness ("No, I don't!"), which blocks further communication. In the second, you are being responsible for your feelings and the other person will be more receptive to hearing what you have to say.

3. Avoid the person altogether. No one can force you to be friends with him or her, so you are free to break away from someone if he or she is consistently a source of stress for you. A polite note or discussion to the effect of "this just isn't working out for me" may be the kindest route to take. Each situation is different though, and you should follow your instincts about what to say as you break away.

Of course, you can't exactly end a relationship with a pesky younger brother or a teacher who gets on your nerves. But you can reduce your interactions by keeping conversations to a minimum—at least until the irritation passes.

4. Analyze *why* you find this person irritating to see if you can simply change your point of view. Is it possible that your thoughts or beliefs about the other person are responsible for your irritation?

Things: Material objects, too, can be sources of irritation and stress, such as a bicycle lock that is difficult to close, an under-powered blowdryer, or a broken backpack that continually falls off your shoulders.

Instead of trying to ignore worn-out, broken, or inadequate items, ask your parents to help you replace them. If your parents complain about the cost, you still should make efforts to fix the situation. Save and use your allowance, if you must, because these little material irritants do add up to some big stress.

A disorderly room, locker, or desk also creates stress. Even if you don't dust and vaccuum every day, try to keep the areas where you store your stuff picked up and tidy.

PRESSURES

Clean your **room! Feed the dog! Keep** your **grades UP!** Sometimes it feels as if you've got a ton of pressure on your head. Now that you're no longer a child, the adults around you expect you to fulfill bigger and greater responsibilities. But help! All of a sudden you're wishing you could revert back to the simpler days of childhood.

Pressure *is* a part of adolescence and adulthood; however, you can considerably reduce its impact by being sure to:

a. *Prioritize.* Know what's important to you and spend most of your time on that project. For example, let's say your top priority is to get a high grade point average. You would then spend a majority of your time fulfilling that priority, such as studying or doing extra credit work.

People feel pressure most when they know, deep down, they're wasting time on something unrelated to their ultimate goals. Even though you may not feel like it, push yourself to complete high-priority tasks *before* you engage in lower-priority activities. Afterward, you will thank yourself!

b. *Know what motivates you.* Are you someone who puts off writing term papers until the night before? Do you tend to study best in a quiet library or in a cozy corner of your room? When you understand the unique way your mind and study habits work together, you can plan ways that will maximize your success. For example, if you tend to procrastinate writing essays until the last minute, you can push yourself to write a little bit on a daily basis.

c. *Create and stick to your personal timetable.* So, you've got three weeks to study for an exam. Instead of feeling an out-of-control pressure about the test, why not take control and organize your study time? On your own calendar write a timetable of studying. For example, write "7–8:00 P.M., study for math test" on each day on the calendar. If you know that you need extra study time on the days or weeks before the big exam, schedule in additional hours of study.

Once you make a **timetable,** *it's important to* **stick to it!**

It's probably impossible to completely avoid stressful situations. And who would want to miss out on positive stressors, such as holidays? As just mentioned, some people use stress and time pressures as a motivator to accomplish their goals.

Still, you're wise to keep stress and its effects to a minimum. After all, you have enough to worry about with adolescence coming your way!

*Y*ou CAN Deal With It!

Take one afternoon a week as your own personal stress-free time. During the period (anywhere from two to six hours), you are not allowed to worry or stress about anything! Instead, do something you normally don't give yourself time to do: rearrange your room, call a grandparent, plant flowers, chase butterflies, whatever makes you happy!

CHAPTER 9

Major Crushes and First Loves

This is crazy! I don't know how I feel, and you're making it harder. What if I did like Sam? Would that be so bad?

— Nancy Drew in *Kiss and Tell*

"Oh my gosh, did you check out that new guy in our first period class!" Bridgette blurted out to her best friend, Lisa. "He's so cute I can't believe it!" Bridgette spun around on her heels and pressed her books up against her chest. "I think I'm in love!" she practically shouted.

Lisa rolled her eyes skyward, then looked at her friend bouncing and dancing across the school lawn. "Bridgette, you're always falling in love," Lisa reminded her. Bridgette turned back to her friend, with a big, goofy grin on her face, and said, "Yeah, but this time it's *for real*!"

Do you know anyone who's like Bridgette? Someone who always has a crush on some guy at school, or some movie star or musician? Are you like that yourself?

Boy-Crazy Crushes

It wasn't that long ago when boys were yucky and full of cooties. Now, you find that your heart skips a beat whenever

 that cute boy says "Hi" to you. You absentmindedly doodle your favorite rock star's name on your notebook. And you dream about kissing that movie star in your sleep. What happened? Did boys just get cuter?

Actually, your body and emotions are preparing you for adulthood and the family that eventually you may choose to have. Most animals, including human beings, form family units. You are most likely drawn to a certain type of boy: You prefer certain personality styles, eye and hair colors, height or body build, and styles of dressing. This is another part of your unique personality.

> . . . you find that your heart skips a beat whenever that cute boy says "Hi" to you.

Some girls like boys who are similar to themselves or family members. This is where the term, "birds of a feather flock together" comes from. But other girls, particularly those who come from troubled households, purposely pick boys who are practically opposite from their family members. Either way, your family has a big influence on the kind of boys you are (or will be) attracted to.

If you have no interest in the opposite sex or seem confused about how you feel, the most important thing you could do is talk about it. If you're like most girls, however, this is exactly the *last* subject you want to discuss with anyone.

Confiding in a counselor, adult friend, or parent, will help you sort out those frustrating (and totally normal) feelings you may be experiencing.

Romantic Personalities

While all humans—male and female—enjoy falling and being in love, studies show that some people are more prone to experiencing romantic love than others. Romantic personality types have the following tendencies and characteristics:

♥ A tendency to **quickly develop and then drop crushes** on various people (may have a crush on four or five different people in one month's time, for example).

♥ When a crush first develops, the romantic personality may believe that, "**This is it!** This is the perfect person for me!"

♥ The **crush fades quickly,** often after the romantic personality discovers that their "perfect person" in fact has some ordinary human "flaw."

♥ In addition, studies reveal that the romantic personality type usually **enjoys being the center of attention**, and having all eyes upon her (or him). She may also be a very dramatic person.

♥ The romantic personality type **loves mushy movies** and romance novels.

There is nothing wrong with being a romantic personality, and you may share one, two, or all of these characteristics yourself. If so, you are likely a girl who loves the idea of being in love. Whether or not you are the romantic type, though, you are likely to have curiosities and questions about boy-girl relationships. Here are some normal worries and concerns, along with heartfelt guidance and answers.

Love Q & A

Q: *How can I tell if I'm really in love?*

A: It's sometimes tough even for adults to tell the difference between having a crush on someone and being in love with someone. Usually, time is the telling factor. Crushes are short-lived and involve a lot of physical responses, such as fluttering heartbeats, difficulty in swallowing, and butterflies in the stomach. Love means that you've taken the time to get to know the other person. Love also means that you respect, care for, and have common interests with the other person.

Q: *The guys at school pay the most attention to girls who dress and act sexy. Sometimes I feel bad about the way I look, and I worry that I'll never have a relationship since guys seem to only care about a girl's looks. Is there anything I can do to stop these feelings, short of dressing and acting like those other girls?*

A: Many sociologists agree with you: Males do put a lot of emphasis on their partner's physical appearance. For instance, brainwave studies suggest that males are more visually-oriented than females, who tend to be more focused on what they hear than on what they see. Other researchers conclude that the male's focus on female attractiveness stems way back to caveman days when men had to quickly assess the health and fertility of cave-women. Some sociologists argue that almost everyone—whether male or female—notices attractive females, or a person dressed in attention-getting clothes.

However, like many females, most guys are also concerned with finding a girl who's pretty on the inside, as well as on the outside. Males want their female companion to have an easygoing personality, a good sense of humor, the ability to communicate well, and some common interests.

. . . it's even more important for you to develop attractive inner traits (such as honesty, loyalty, and development of your talents) that help you have a great relationship with yourself.

Worries about your appearance are normal, especially as your figure undergoes significant maturation changes. Taking good care of your physical health through proper nutrition, rest, good hygiene, and exercise boosts your confidence about your outer self. But it's even more important for you to develop attractive inner traits (such as honesty, loyalty, and development of your talents) that help you have a great relationship with yourself. Only then can you attract and maintain a guy worthy of your time and attention.

Q: *Help! I'm really confused about what to do. A guy I really like says that if I make out with him, he'll be my steady boyfriend. I'm afraid that if I don't do what he wants, he'll* *stop seeing me altogether. But I'm also upset because he's moving way too fast for me. What should I do?*

A: First, you should never do anything you don't feel comfortable with. If that means breaking up with the boy, do it! You also need to know that making out—kissing and hugging—can lead to more intense and intimate encounters, experiences you aren't prepared to handle emotionally.

Q: *My brother says all guys want is sex. I can't believe it. Why would a guy say he loves me, if he doesn't?*

A: For boys, making out is mostly a physical, rather than an emotional, experience. Teenage boys are going through powerful hormonal changes that make them want to have sexual experiences. On the other hand, for most girls, making out leads to romantic feelings. So, boys often say lines to girls in order to pressure them into agreeing to go further sexually than they might feel comfortable doing. Some of the more common lines include:

> "I'll break up with you if you won't have sex with me."

> "We're going to get married someday, so it's okay to have sex."

> "If you really loved me, you'd want to please me by going all the way."

Don't believe any of these lines for a moment! Any guy who has to manipulate a girl in order to gain physical affection is not a true-blue guy. Most guys who use lines on girls are not prepared for steady relationships; he may make out with one girl on Friday and another girl on

Saturday. It's not worth the heartache and possible physical disease or pregnancy, just because of a desire to please an unpleasable guy.

Sex is a very complicated topic with many emotional and physical implications. The book, *Your Body, Yourself,* is a good resource for learning more about sexuality.

Q: *Sometimes I feel depressed because I really like this one guy at school, but he barely ever notices me. Is it okay for a girl to ask a guy for his phone number?*

A: Every guy is different. Some guys are thrilled to have a girl approach him; while others are turned off by it. Your best approach is to show you're interested in him by smiling and saying, "Hi." If you really want to talk to him or ask him out, then that's a part of your personality you shouldn't try to hide. After all, the guy who's right for you is a guy who wouldn't be offended or afraid of your true personality. You might as well be yourself around him from the beginning!

Q: *A girl at school always teases me because I'm a virgin. This really upsets me, and makes me feel like a freak because so many girls at school have gone all the way. Am I a geek to still be a virgin?*

A: Not at all, although your worries are quite normal. *Many cool girls and guys believe that virginity should be saved for the wedding night.* It is considered a gift to one's self and one's spouse, as well as a way to avoid sexually-transmitted diseases and pregnancy. In addition, most people are better able to handle the deep responsibilities and emotions that accompany sexual intercourse when they are old enough to get married. The enjoyment of sexual intercourse is also greatly enhanced by the deep bond, trust, and love that you'll no doubt have with your future husband.

Q: *Even though my boyfriend and I broke up two months ago, I can't stop thinking about him. How can I get over him?*

A: It takes awhile to recover from the breakup of a relationship, especially if this was your first love. The circumstances surrounding the end can also determine the amount of healing time your heart will need. If he broke up with you, or if you caught him cheating on you, the feelings of loss are compounded by other painful feelings of humiliation, betrayal, or anger. Give yourself some time.

You can speed up the healing process by avoiding contact with him, as well as any songs, places, or movies that remind you of him—at least for a while. Before you know it, the tune that used to be "your song" is just another fun melody to dance to. Talk to a trusted friend to get the feelings off your chest. Or, in your journal, write five reasons why he's the wrong guy for you, in addition to writing about your various feelings connected to the breakup.

Try not to spend too much time isolated in your bedroom, and don't waste time moping around. Instead, get out there and get active! Start a hobby, make a new friend, or join a sports team. Whatever you do, though, don't jump into a new romantic relationship right away. Give your emotions some time to heal, or else your grief could contaminate any new relationship.

Q: *I told my best friend that I had a crush on this guy in our fifth period class. Now she's flirting with him like crazy, and she's trying to get him to notice her. Should I quit being her friend?*

> **Whatever you do, though, don't jump into a new romantic relationship right away.**

A: One of the reasons you and your girlfriend became friends in the first place was because of your shared interests and likes. It's normal that you and she would like the same kind of guy! However, most friends have unspoken agreements that they won't compete for one another's boyfriend. Before you clobber her for betraying your friendship, have a talk with her to make sure she really understood you when you told her about your feelings for the guy. A true friend will back off from a guy once she discovers her buddy had feelings for him first. If your pal insists on going for him anyway, then you should take a close look at the nature of your friendship.

Q: *I like two guys at the same time. How is that possible?*

A: When you first start noticing the opposite sex, you are attracted to a wide variety of factors. In one guy, you may be attracted to his physical appearance and admire his similarity to your favorite television actor. Another guy

may attract you because he's got a warm, outgoing personality. With each guy for whom you develop feelings, you
learn more and more about your own likes and dislikes.
Staying aware of these things is how you learn about yourself. This self-knowledge will eventually help you choose a
compatible marriage partner.

In the meantime, take steps to keep yourself out of any
messy love triangles. For instance, avoid lying to one boy
in order to spend time with the other. If you're not sure
that you're ready to commit one hundred percent to just
one guy, be upfront about your feelings with possible
steady boyfriends. By being honest with yourself and others, you're less apt to feel upset or confused if you like
more than one guy at a time.

You CAN Deal With It!

Talk to your mom or grandma about some of her dating relationships in the past. What was her first kiss like? How did
she meet her husband? You'll certainly learn a few things
about love, and you may see your mother or grandmother in a
whole new light!

CHAPTER 10

ℱriendships and Feelings

My best friend, Carly, and I fight sometimes. But then one of us ends up calling the other one, and pretty soon we're best friends again.

— Nikki Colovich, age 14, Corpus Christi, Texas

𝒜s you get older and spend more time away from home, it's natural that your friendships will change, develop, and deepen. Friendships are filled with intense emotions, both positive and negative. The level of friendship will depend on the amount of intimacy shared between two people.

ACQUAINTANCES

Acquaintances are people whom you know, but may not necessarily socialize with. You may have an occasional conversation or shared event with an acquaintance, but usually the relationship is limited to "hello" and "goodbye." For example, the girl who sits next to you in math class or the guy with the locker next to yours could be considered acquaintances.

You'll have hundreds, maybe thousands, of acquaintances during your lifetime. As you make changes in your life, such as going to college, getting a job, moving, or getting married, you'll gain and lose acquaintances.

FRIENDS

A friend is different from an acquaintance for two main reasons. First, you willingly spend free time with a friend, because you enjoy the person's company. Second, you and your friend are willing to do things for one another. For example, if your bicycle was broken, your friend would loan you hers for the day. Or if your friend was sad because her boyfriend didn't call, you'd console her and help her feel better.

BEST FRIENDS

Extremely close friends are called "best friends." They share secrets and much of their free time. A best friend is someone who gives you advice, encouragement, companionship, and understanding all at the same time.

Friendship Feelings

Developing friendships is an important part of growing up because it teaches us how to interact with other people. Here are a few of the virtues most of us learn from our friendships:

HONESTY

All friendships have moments where people disagree. Let's say that you are furious with your friend Sandy. **What do you do?**

a *You could hide your feelings.* This doesn't work because Sandy won't know about your true feelings and the same argument is bound to recur.

b *You could blast her with anger.* This would create unnecessary ill feelings. While it's healthy to express your feelings, it's not a good idea to do so in a hurtful manner.

c *You could assertively discuss your feelings.* This is a great idea, because you are opening up to Sandy about your true feelings and thoughts. If she accepts you as you are and respects your opinions, then you know she's a friend. Friendship means that two people genuinely know and like one another. The only way Sandy can be your true friend is if you allow her to know the real you.

SETTING BOUNDARIES

Your new friend, Laura, is really cool. The only trouble is she always wants to borrow things from you, such as money, CDs, and clothes. Plus, she doesn't return the borrowed items unless you continually remind her!

Whenever you enter into a new relationship, you must teach the other person about what is acceptable and what is unacceptable behavior for you. This is called "setting boundaries." Every person's boundaries vary depending on what fits his or her needs. If Laura hopes to keep you as a friend, she must learn that her borrowing habits are unacceptable to you.

The only way she can learn this is by you *clearly* telling her. In other words, don't just drop hints about your feelings—that's not enough. Sit Laura down and tell her, nicely but directly, about your boundaries concerning friendships.

Most people discover what behavior they will and won't accept from others through experiences. Each friendship helps you to learn more about your likes and dislikes.

LOYALTY

You're gossiping with a group of girls, when the topic of discussion turns to your best friend Allison. The girls are saying really mean things about her! Do you:

a Join in the discussion and tell the group about Allison's embarrassing secrets.

b Listen quietly.

c Leave the room.

d Stand up for her and defend her reputation.

Friendship often brings up issues of loyalty and betrayal. In the example above, **a** is an example of betrayal; **b** is also betrayal because your silence implies that you endorse the gossip about Allison; **c** shows more loyalty; and **d** shows the most loyalty.

Sometimes you might worry that your friend likes another person more than she likes you. At those times, it's normal to feel worried or jealous. Healthy steps to take in these situations are to, first, write your feelings in your private journal, so that you're clear about your thoughts. Second, once you understand what you feel and why, you're ready to have an honest and assertive discussion with your friend. As discussed earlier, don't put your friend on the defensive. Tell her how you feel, not what she is doing wrong.

While it's helpful to understand what made you upset, remember that you have the right to feel any emotion that comes to you. You never need to justify or apologize about anything you are feeling (although you may need to apologize if you *act thoughtlessly* in response to an emotion). They are your emotions, they belong to you, and they are perfectly natural.

Also, keep in mind that the issue of loyalty in friendship goes both ways. True friends stand up for one another, trust one another, and are sensitive to one another's feelings.

> **True friends** stand up for one another, trust one another, and are sensitive to one another's feelings.

Loneliness

Have you ever been lonely, feeling as if there was nothing to do and no one to talk to? It's a feeling that many teenagers experience from time to time. Part of loneliness comes from all the changes you are experiencing. Loneliness can also come from:

Holding negative thoughts that push people away. For example, feeling that no one likes you or that no one cares. Negativity repels people, while a positive attitude attracts friends like a magnet.

Staying isolated. Many people are lonely because they stay alone. There are plenty of ways to meet new friends, if you push yourself a little. Join an after-school club, a church or youth group, get a part-time job, or become a part of a sports team. Go to where people are—*that's* the first step in becoming part of a group of friends.

Acting anti-social. Behavior that pushes others away includes being bossy, bragging or showing off, dressing or acting outrageously weird, and being dishonest.

While it's true that you should be yourself around others, it's also necessary to develop social skills such as friendliness, warmth, honesty, and respect for others. Anyone can learn how to be a good friend. One secret to being popular among your friends is developing good listening skills. *(See "Six Secrets of Super Listeners" on the following page.)*

Pressures of Popularity

We all want to be treated with respect. It's only natural! But sometimes, we want even more: We want to be like those

SIX SECRETS OF SUPER LISTENERS

Good listeners are always popular and in demand. Perhaps you've met a good listener, and have been impressed that they heard and understood the true meaning of your words and feelings. Here are the six secrets of good listeners:

DO concentrate on the other person's words, instead of thinking of what you'll say in reply.

DON'T offer advice, suggestions, or criticisms unless specifically invited to do so.

DO make appropriate eye contact as the other person is speaking. Studies show that most people look at the person speaking eighty percent of the time, and look away the balance of the time. You don't want to stare; you just want to show that you are paying attention.

DON'T insist on turning the topic of conversation toward yourself.

DO say, "Uh—hmm" or nod occasionally to indicate you are listening.

DO briefly summarize what you heard the other person say so you *know* you are understanding her.

Even though you may be set on being the greatest listener ever, don't forget that even super listeners need people to listen to them spout off, too!

super-cool girls and guys. We want to be popular. Popularity means that most of the kids at school know your name, and that they want to hang around you. Kids gain popularity in a number of different ways, including:

❀ Developing super-listening and other social skills.

❀ Being highly visible as a student body president, a cheer-leader, a musician, or a sports star.

❀ Possessing extreme physical beauty, or dressing extraordinarily fashionable.

❀ Having something that others want, like a car, swimming pool, or house where friends are always welcome.

Many times, popularity looks like more fun than it actually is. Just because a person has a lot of admirers and acquaintances does not necessarily mean that he or she is a happy person. This is especially true when the popular person is involved in unhealthy lifestyles, such as drugs or gangs. It is impossible to have negative habits and feel deep, true happiness.

> We all want respect, but sometimes, we want even more: We want to be like those super-cool girls and guys. We want to be *popular.*

At one time or another, you'll probably be confronted with a situation where someone asks you to do something that you know is wrong. A guy will say, "If you have sex, I'll be your boyfriend," or a girl will say, "If you smoke pot with us, you can join our group."

 How will you handle such pressures of popularity? Through the questions below, you can begin to form your personal philosophy on values concerning popularity pressures. (You may not have an easy answer to any of these questions. Take as much time as you need to think and discuss your opinions with friends before drawing any conclusions.)

✗ *Do I believe it's ever okay to use illegal drugs?*

✗ Do I believe it's ever justifiable to steal from another person? How about stealing from a store?

✗ **Do I believe it's ever okay to laugh, tease, or make fun of another person?**

✗ When it comes to physical affection and sex, am I ready for all the intense physical and emotional consequences? Am I prepared to say *"no"* in the face of pressure to say *"yes"*?

✗ *Do I believe that cheating, lying, or telling half-truths is ever justifiable? When is lying not okay? How would I hurt myself and others by lying?*

✗ How will I handle it when other kids are pressuring me to do something that I know is wrong?

✗ **How would it affect my self-esteem if I did something I knew was wrong?**

✗ *How would my parents react if they discovered my wrong behavior?*

You Are Your Own Best Friend

Happiness comes from acting in ways that are healthy and

that enhance your life. There's an old saying that sums this up perfectly: "Wherever you go, there you are." This means that you can try and only please other people, or you can try and run away from problems, but in the end you have to stand up and please yourself.

The years of adolescence are a perfect time to develop a close friendship with the most important person you'll ever know: you. Be true to yourself, and never compromise your values just to gain popularity. This doesn't mean that you should be selfish or only think about your own feelings. Instead, it means learn how to maintain a healthy respect for yourself, while at the same time being kind and honest to those around you. It's a winning combination!

You CAN Deal With It!

Evaluate what kind of friend you are.

- When your friend asks you something, do you always answer honestly?

- Do you try to help your friend when she is down, or do you just leave her alone until her "mood" passes?

- Have you ever told your friend how special she is?

How do you know if you answered correctly? How would you want your friends to answer each question? You should always try to treat others the way you want to be treated!

CHAPTER 11

*F*amily and Feelings

> "Young lady, you do what your mother says and you do it now. She shouldn't have to tell you three times," said Mr. Quimby.
>
> "Well, all right, but you don't have to be so cross," said Ramona. To herself she thought, <u>Nag, nag, nag.</u>
>
> — Ramona Quimby,
> in Beverly Cleary's *Ramona and Her Father*

*N*ow that you're getting older, your relationships with your family are probably changing. You may feel closer than you used to to certain family members, such as your dad or older sibling. But other people in your family may suddenly seem super-irritating to you, as if they're on a special mission to make you miserable.

Here are some guidelines to why and how your family affects your emotions, as well as some ways to keep your relationship with, and feelings about, your family running smoothly.

Why Do My Parents Act This Way?

When you were little, your parents seemed like the smartest people in the world. How come all of a sudden they seem so old-fashioned to you? One reason is that you are starting to see that your parents are people with human flaws and quirks, and not the perfect grown-ups they once seemed to be.

As you grow older, you'll naturally be replacing childhood dependencies with self-responsibilities. As you read earlier, the process of separation-individuation is one of the most important (and, for you and your parents, emotionally painful) parts of being a teenager.

There will be times when you wished you lived all by yourself, *and other times when you want to cuddle up in your mother's lap.*

As with any new venture, this natural process of separating from your parents will create changes between you and your parents that may feel clumsy or awkward in the beginning. There will be times when you wished you lived all by yourself, and other times when you want to cuddle up in your mother's lap. Also, at times you'll insist on making all your own decisions for yourself, and the next moment, you'll feel incapable of deciding anything on your own. One minute your parents' opinions are worthless, the next they're invaluable.

Beginning to see the see-saw pattern? Don't get too frustrated. As you and your folks grow accustomed to your increasing independence, the ups and downs will eventually smooth out.

My Parents Treat Me Like a Baby!

One of the greatest frustrations is feeling like your parents still see you as a little girl. Here you are, almost grown up, and your mom talks to you as if you were a five-year-old! *Grrrrrr!*

There are two main solutions to this problem. First, know that your parents will give you more respect and trust as they see you acting like an adult. *What does that mean?* It means being responsible and holding yourself accountable to keeping promises you make, being on time, and doing your chores.

Second, be careful to talk to your parents as you'd want them to talk to you—*in a calm, low-key, and respectful manner.* Some teenagers express their frustration toward their parents with loud sighs and smart-aleck comments. Unfortunately, those methods always backfire! The more aggressive the tone of voice and the choice of words, the more parents view their daughter as being immature.

This issue of being treated like a little girl is tough to deal with, to be sure! But with patience, persistence, and a commitment to act grown up on your part, it will naturally resolve itself.

PHONE LINES

You've got so many new friends, and you're anxious to spend time with them. You and your pals love to chat on the phone, but your mom says you talk too long. *What to do?*

Some girls use their allowance or baby-sitting money to pay for their own telephone line. But a phone is an expensive responsibility, and your parents may not approve right away. As with other things that you want, ask your parents if there are specific guidelines that they'd agree to. For example, perhaps they'd get you a telephone if you saved up thirty or forty dollars that they could hold as a "deposit" against your telephone bills.

Another solution is to negotiate certain times when you can use the phone. Maybe your parents will let you talk after your homework is finished, from 7:30 to 8:00 P.M., for example. Whatever you and your family come up with, it's important to demonstrate your maturity by listening to their opinions. If you don't agree with them, then share your thoughts in an intelligent, assertive manner. You'll win their respect and their cooperation!

CARS, CARS, CARS

In addition to chatting via the phone lines with your friends, you also want to hang out with them in person. Maybe you even know someone (like a friend's older brother) who has a driver's license and access to a car. But the trouble is, your parents won't let you ride with him and your friend.

As with the telephone, it will take time and effort to earn your parents' trust. It may help to see your parents' point of view: Your mom and dad aren't being mean when they tell you "no." They're being protective. They are afraid you'll be hurt or killed in an auto accident. It's not necessarily that they don't trust you, but they know that teenaged drivers have less experience.

Here are some guidelines for dealing with the whole car issue, both to earn your parents' trust and to ensure your own safety while driving or riding in a car:

Do keep all your promises when your parents allow you to ride in a friend's car. This includes maintaining your curfew, and always buckling your seat belt.

Don't ever ride in a car with a driver who's been drinking. It isn't worth the high risk of a deadly auto accident.

Do make sure the car you ride in is in good operating condition, and that it has safe brakes, tires, and sufficient fuel.

Don't hesitate to tell the driver of your car to slow down. Speeding and reckless driving are major causes of death among adolescents and young adults.

Brothers and Sisters

In addition to keeping peace with your parents, you probably have siblings living with you. You're likely experiencing intense changes in your relationships with your brothers and sisters. This is especially true with siblings who are five or more years younger or older than you. Yet, even only a few years in age difference can make siblings feel totally unable to relate to one another.

Feelings of jealousy and rivalry between siblings spoil many girls' teenage years. But believe it or not, siblings also serve a very important and useful function in your psychological and developmental growth! Your brothers and sisters have enormous influence upon the shaping of your personality and behavioral habits.

Many times, people purposely decide to be the complete and total opposite of a sibling. For instance, your sister is a slob, so you strive to be ultra neat in an effort to be very different from her. By creating a personality characteristic that is 180 degrees opposite of a sibling, you engage in "**de-identification**." This means that you shape your identity in response to another person, but instead of modeling their behavior, you go in the other direction.

Let's take a look at some common problems and ways of dealing with your younger and older brothers and sisters.

LITTLE SISTERS

She admires and envies you, and sometimes it seems like she's out to make your life miserable! She's your kid sister, and—especially if she's several years younger than you—your relationship is probably emotionally intense and complicated.

For instance, you can't help but feel protective about her. After all, you can remember being her age and you want to shield her from life's problems. But it's awful when mom forces you to baby-sit her on the days when you want to be with your friends.

Fortunately, there are some things you can do to make life easier for both of you.

First, understand your sister's point of view. She wants to be older, like you. She also wants your attention and respect—which is a big compliment to you. So, when she uses your makeup or tries on your shoes, she's really not *trying* to ruin your possessions. **What can you do to keep your sanity?** Put together a box of old clothes and makeup for her to play with. She'll adore you for it, and you won't have to worry as much about what she's touching in your room.

Instead of yelling at her when she acts like a brat, you can prevent her from acting bratty in the first place. Here's how: Give her ten minutes of undivided attention each and every day. Also, whenever you see her do something good like draw or color a picture or build something with her blocks, let her know you recognize how wonderful she is. This little investment on your part is minor compared to the amount of peace—and love—you'll reap as a reward.

LITTLE BROTHERS

Like a little sister, he desperately wants your attention and wishes he was older, like you. But a little brother is more likely to try to get your attention by annoying you.

You can ask your parents for help if your little brother is being extremely rude. But you can also do a lot to prevent your brother's irritating actions by giving him a little undivided attention on a regular basis. That way, he won't feel the need to get your attention by annoying you.

OLDER SISTERS

She's so busy and sometimes very bossy. She's your older sister and you've got lots of strong feelings about how she treats you. At times, she waves you off like you're nothing but a pesky kid. At other times, she expects you to do all of her chores and special favors. *What gives?*

In a way, you desperately want her friendship and approval, because—you hate to admit it, but—**you think she's pretty cool.**

You likely have lots of interwoven thoughts and feelings about your big sister, many of them painful. In a way, you desperately want her friendship and approval, because—you hate to admit it, but—you think she's pretty cool. In fact, you often try to be like her. But then you get mad at yourself, and at her, when she makes fun of the way you dress and act.

Even though a part of you wants to hug her and another part of you wants to bop her on the head, do yourself a big, big favor by trying to keep the peace. One step toward getting along with Big Sis (as with everyone else) is to understand her point of view. She's also going through growing pains as she gets older. And if it seems unfair that your folks give her extra privileges, remember that she also has extra responsibilities.

The bottom line is: Don't take her actions too personally. Tell her how you feel, honestly and assertively, but also be sure to give her the quiet, personal time she needs.

OLDER BROTHERS

He tries to protect you by telling you which guys to date and which to stay away from. The trouble is, he wants you to stay away from all the really cute guys! If you're upset because your big brother is acting more like a drill sergeant, don't despair.

Instead, try to see things from his perspective: He knows that guys often try to take advantage of girls. He listens to guys bragging about how far they've gone sexually with certain girls, and your big brother doesn't want these guys to take advantage of you!

Your brother really believes that he's doing you a favor by being protective. But if you think he's going too far, explain your point of view to him. Once he sees that you are becoming an assertive young lady, and are not a helpless little girl, he'll back off a bit.

STEP AND HALF SIBLINGS

If your parents have divorced and remarried, you may have brothers and sisters who aren't related to you by blood. This is called a "blended family," a structure that is increasingly commonplace in our society. A step-brother or sister is related to you only by marriage, while a half-brother or sister shares either the same mother or father with you.

Your feelings about your parents' divorce will influence your feelings about the new members of your family. It's important to give your step-brothers and step-sisters a fair shake, and not blame them for your parents' divorce. After all, their parents went through a divorce, too! Try to separate your feelings toward step-siblings from the feelings you have about your parents. Who knows, you may actually find that your step-sibling can provide you with a new source of friendship, support, and understanding!

114∽ Your Emotions, Yourself

Changes Outside Your Control

Like you, your parents go through periods of emotional strain. Sometimes, a teen's emotional changes are triggered by such dramatic shifts in family circumstances. Divorce, the death of a family member, moving to a strange city, or financial problems, can all upset the family balance and your parents' state of mind. **Where everything used to be so nice and happy, you may now find that suddenly your parents are in bad, really bad, moods.**

It's important not to blame yourself if your parents are experiencing stressful times. Just as you are in charge of the ways that you deal with painful emotions, your parents must take control over and deal with their feelings.

When Parents Divorce

Every year, thousands of families are torn apart by divorce. Perhaps your own family has gone through this painful process. Sometimes, children are relieved because a divorce means an end to horrible parental arguments. But always, divorce carries strong feelings that are often confusing to understand. Here are some emotions which accompany divorce.

SHOCK AND FEAR

At first, you can't believe your ears. *Your parents are really splitting up?* It feels as if your whole world is crumbling to pieces. You're numb and in shock. Then, you start to feel afraid. What if I never see my father again? What if Mom marries some cruel, creepy man?

It's important that you talk to someone about these feelings.

Anyone experiencing a life crisis, like parental divorce, benefits from emotional support. Your mom and dad may be preoccupied with their own strong thoughts right now. So, unfortunately, they may not be available to help you deal with your feelings. If this is the case, talk with a trusted teacher, school counselor, nurse, clergy person, girl scout leader, or a friend's parents.

Or ask your parents to make an appointment for you to see a professional counselor. They can provide anyone with emotional support during times of turmoil and life crisis. In the meantime, know that these feelings are temporary and you won't always feel this bad.

SELF-BLAME/GUILT

Many kids blame themselves for their parents' divorce. "If I had been a better girl, Dad wouldn't have left Mom," is how many children think. But there's no way that a divorce is caused by children, even if it seems like all their arguments used to be about you or your brothers and sisters. Divorce is a complicated decision that adults make when they cannot work together with love, respect, and mutual goals. There are a million reasons why parents get a divorce, and it's silly to think that you are at fault for something so complicated. That's like blaming yourself for the weather or the economy. Don't do it!

ANGER

"Why did my parents have to get a divorce in the first place?" "Why did this have to happen to ME?" "Why can't my parents get back together again?" These are some natural questions that most children of divorce ask themselves. Heal yourself from the pain of anger by talking about your feelings with your parents. Believe it or not, your parents also benefit from an honest discussion about emotions.

SADNESS / DEPRESSION

It's also normal to feel sad when your parents divorce. After all, you probably miss the parent you no longer live with. You wish your family still ate meals together and did other normal things that two-parent families do. Although it may seem like the end of the world when your parents divorce, there are ways to pull yourself out of a blue mood. Chapter 12 is filled with effective ways to achieve the happiness you deserve.

FRUSTRATION

Child custody arrangements usually involve visitations. Maybe you see your Dad every other weekend, or perhaps you spend the summer with him. These visits bring up a lot of strong emotions, don't they?

Even little things like forgetting to bring the brown shoes that go with your jeans outfit or leaving your toothpaste at home can be frustrating. More important, there is also the awkwardness of Mom and Dad meeting when they drop you off. How should you act? Will they start fighting? You probably just wish they would get back together again.

It may help you to know these are normal feelings. Take your journal with you on visits, so that you can handle your feelings as needed. Write about the activities you and your parent participate in, and record all the happy and not-so-happy experiences and conversations that come up during your visit. List five reasons why you feel close to both your parents, and list five things you'd like to do with your noncustodial parent (the parent you don't live with most of the time) on future visits. Be sure to share these hopes and plans with your parent, so he or she can know what's on your mind.

It also helps if you ask the noncustodial parent to have a little private cabinet or chest of drawers for your visits. That way, you can keep a second set of clothes and toiletry items at his or her house. The more things you can do to make yourself feel at home, the easier it'll be for you to manage.

Serious Family Problems

Sometimes adults do or say things that seriously hurt their children's bodies or self-esteem. This behavior is called "child abuse," and it is both illegal and a violation of a child's personal rights. If you, or someone you know, has suffered from one of these forms of child abuse, don't delay reporting the abuse to a trusted parent, your teacher, school counselor or nurse, or one of the hotlines listed in the back of this book. Depending on the situation, these adults and professionals may need to take drastic

Sometimes

that seriously

adults do

hurt their children's

or say

bodies or self-esteem.

things

steps to intervene, such as removing the abused child from a violent and dangerous household. In most cases, child abuse can be treated through a combination of individual and family counseling that helps both parents and the child heal their related psychological problems.

Psychological abuse

When adults consistently belittle their children it is called "psychological abuse." Some kids are raised in families in which parents or caretakers continually say negative things about the child's abilities, intelligence, or appearance. Phrases such as, "You're no good," "You'll never amount to anything," or "Quit being such a stupid idiot," often come out of the mouths of parents who actually think they are helping their children. Unfortunately, children usually believe these phrases to be true. Then they grow up believing they are inferior human beings.

Neglect

Children depend upon their parents or guardians to provide for their needs: food, clothing, shelter, and protection. When parents fail to provide these basic physical needs for their children, it is a form of child abuse called "neglect." Another form of neglect is when parents don't spend much time talking, interacting, or showing affection and love for their children.

Physical Abuse

Way beyond spankings and discipline, physical abuse involves inflicting pain or injury on the child.

The abuse can include intense spankings, whippings, bruises, cuts, forced cigarette burns, starvation, broken bones, and even death. Parents who physically abuse their children are often alcoholic, drug addicted, or mentally ill. Usually, they suffered abuse when they were small children, and are perpetuating the family cycle of violence. If you know a young person who has suspicious and unexplainable black eyes, bruises, or broken bones, talk to him or her. Often, abuse survivors feel ashamed about discussing their violent home life, fearing that you will think less of them for it. But if you assure the abuse survivor that you are trying to help, you could potentially avert a tragedy.

SEXUAL ABUSE

This involves forcing or coercing the child to engage in sexual acts with an adult. Sexual abuse occurs in families of all economic, religious, racial, and social backgrounds. As with other forms of abuse, the victim feels intense shame about admitting and discussing her sexual abuse experiences. She often blames herself for not stopping the abuse, not realizing that the adult abuser is entirely responsible. Unless she gets counseling or understands that she's not at fault for the abuse, her self-blame results in severely low self-esteem. Sexual abuse survivors often act in self-destructive ways, including addictions, promiscuity, shoplifting, dropping out of school, and running away from home.

Parental Psychological Problems

It's clear that any adult who abuses a child is in need of professional help. What's not so clear are other cases where the child suspects that something is wrong with his or her parent, but doesn't know whom to turn to for help.

Sometimes, parents get caught up in their problems and can't see the detrimental effect their behavior is having on their own, and their family's, lives. If you see your parent behaving in a self-destructive way, such as abusing alcohol or drugs, or behaving as if they are seriously depressed, you should describe your worries to your school nurse or a hotline counselor. He or she can listen to your specific situation, and give advice relevant to you and your parent.

Although you're not yet an adult, you still have feelings and opinions about your parents' behaviors. They definitely have legal and moral responsibilities to uphold within their parental role. If things at your home, or a friend's home, are seriously affected by a parent's irresponsible behavior, then it's up to you to seek help from a responsible adult. You can take charge of your life and make sure you're taken care of and protected.

You CAN
Deal With It!

Describe the biggest fight you had with a family member. How did you handle it? Was the problem resolved? If not, how can you take the first step to fix the relationship? If the problem was resolved, write down how you and the family member did it.

Keep this as a "reference" to look to for help with future family conflicts.

CHAPTER 12

ℱeeling Good About Yourself

"The main thing," Molly said one afternoon, "is to have a good attitude."

Evie made a face.

"No, I'm serious," Molly said. "If you're friendly, cheerful and enthusiastic about stuff, they won't even notice if you put your elbows on the table or forget to shake hands."

— Molly Stewart
in Gabrielle Charbounct's *Princess: A Room in the Attic*

When was the last time you felt good—really good—about yourself? Do you want to reduce stress and increase self-aware-ness and a positive self-image? Just follow the techniques in this chapter! These are methods many adults use with great suc-cess, and who knows? If you try these activities, your friends may ask you to share your secrets for staying so happy!

You may want to try each technique to see which one best suits your personality. These techniques are most effective when used on a regular basis; however, they also work to avert emotional crises. As always, don't hesitate to ask for help from an adult if you start to feel angry, sad, or confused feelings are getting out of your control.

JOURNALING

As discussed throughout, journaling is very effective in reducing confusion, anxiety, and depression, since it helps you to both express and understand what you are feeling, and the reasons why.

DREAM JOURNALING

Similar to journaling, this technique involves keeping a record of your dreams, instead of your emotions. To do so, put a pad of paper and pen next to your bed and get in the habit of writing whatever you can remember about your dreams as soon as you awaken. In the beginning, you'll only remember a fraction of your dreams (everyone has dreams every night, even if you can't recall them). But as you get into a habit of **dream journaling**, you'll be able to remember more and more of your dreams on a regular basis.

Most psychologists and sleep researchers believe that dreams are a series of symbols that show our true thoughts and feelings. For example, if you're feeling confused in algebra class, you may have a dream about walking through a forest that has numbers growing from the tree branches. While there are many books that claim to list the meaning of dream symbols, most experts agree that each symbol is highly personalized.

Usually, as you're writing your dream in your journal, you'll just instinctively know what the dream means to you. ·

DEEP RELAXATION

This technique requires a quiet place where you'll be uninterrupted for at least ten minutes. Sit upright in a comfortable position and close your eyes. Take three deep breaths, inhaling through your nose and holding your breath for at least ten seconds. Then exhale slowly through your mouth.

Continue to breath in and out very deeply as you concentrate on the sounds of your breathing and your heart rate. Probably, you'll notice that they both slow down. Then, contract the muscles in your toes very tightly. Next, let them go. Go up to your calf (lower leg) muscles and clench them tightly. And let them go.

Clench and relax your entire body in this way, moving up from your toes and through each muscle group, all the way to your jaw and forehead. Once you are completely relaxed, you can either focus your mind on a problem you desire to solve or you can concentrate on feel-good thoughts, such as "I can be, do, or have whatever I concentrate upon."

AFFIRMATIONS

What happens when you think a sad thought? Usually, you feel sad! So, is the reverse also true? Does thinking happy thoughts create happy emotions? Yes! Our thoughts definitely affect the way we feel.

Most of us, at one time or another, have had a negative

thought about ourselves. For example, if you dropped food in the crowded school cafeteria, you might have told yourself, "I am so clumsy!" When these kind of negative phrases are thought habitually, self-image and self-esteem suffer.

To reduce or eliminate these negative self-thoughts, you can replace them with positive thoughts. This process is called *"affirmation."* It stems from the word "affirm," which means to declare something as being good. Many mental health professionals prescribe the use of affirmations for raising self-esteem and confidence.

Here's how to do it: Read aloud the following list of affirmations once or twice a day. You may want to copy the list and put it on your bedpost or bathroom mirror. As you're reading the list, notice any negative thoughts that may pop up

Affirmations

I am a good friend and others like me.

I deserve good things to happen to me.

I expect, and receive, good results.

I am smart and I easily learn new information.

My family and I get along together well.

I am successful in everything I do.

I take very good care of myself, and I look and feel great.

I am loved, lovable, and loving.

My body and thoughts obey my every command.

My grades and test scores are improving every day.

My today and future look very bright.

in opposition to the positive thought. For example, a typical negative thought would be, "This is stupid! This won't work on me; maybe on others, but I'm hopeless!" These thoughts are normal in the beginning, and they show only one thing: a definite need for positive thoughts and affirmations.

After reading the affirmations for two weeks, you'll notice an increase in your self-confidence. Regular use of the affirmations for one month creates amazing results. Usually, you'll find that you spontaneously begin to have regular positive thoughts about yourself throughout the day. And because you're thinking positively, you begin to attract more friends and opportunities into your life. You *are* the winner that you know you are!

VISUALIZATION

In **visualization**, you literally reprogram your expectations to match what you want and expect out of life. Here's how:

1. *Decide* exactly what you want a certain situation (sporting event, dance, final exam, future occupation, etc.) to be and look like, including its final outcome involving you.

2. *Write* this description in complete detail.

3. Close your eyes and *imagine* that picture being true right now. Note: this is the tricky part. In order for this technique to really work, you have to concentrate on how you want the situation to look and *refuse* to think about how you're worried it may turn out.

4. *Believe* that this visualization will occur. You can use affirmations, such as "I get good grades on all my tests," "I win the student election," or whatever will help increase

your confidence. But you've got to *believe* that these affirmations will come true. By truly believing in your goals, you will be motivated to work toward them.

With practice, you'll be able to feel more in control of yourself and your life events with the use of this technique. The main point is, *"Expect the best!"*

Lifestyles Leading to Positive Emotions

In addition to self-help techniques, you'll want to incorporate a lifestyle that will boost your healthy self-esteem.

HANG OUT WITH "UP" PEOPLE

Your friends' moods can be contagious, so try to spend as much time as possible with positive, cheerful people. This doesn't mean dumping friends who have an occasional bad day or unfortunate life circumstance. But you don't want to spend a lot of time with people who have any of the habitual negative attitudes, such as the ones below:

Chronic complainers. These people blame everyone but themselves for all their problems. In this way, they don't need to take responsibility for making an effort or decision.

Needy users. These folks don't want a friendship, they want an opportunity to fulfill their own needs. Needy users are eager to talk about themselves, but don't want to hear anything about *your* wishes and desires.

Dulldroms. Have you ever met someone who complained about being bored all the time? You offer suggestions that she could do this or try that, but each time she answers with,

"Yes, but . . ." excuses. She is a "dulldrom," someone trapped in a feeling that there's nothing exciting to do, and that it's too much trouble to do anything to change it.

Stuck-ups. These insecure people try to boost their self-esteem by putting down the rest of the world. A stuck-up person may try to coax you into seeing the world through her eyes with negative phrases such as, "Look at those losers over there." Careful! Though you might feel you're joining an exclusive club by getting close to a stuck-up, you may find yourself adopting her negative and condescending attitudes. And *that* won't do anything for your other friendships, will it?

Doomsayers. These are people who expect the worst in all situations. They are always predicting disasters and problems, and—because they hold such negative thoughts—they often experience problems.

Schemers. Instead of doing the necessary work to improve their grades or make money, these people spend lots of time dreaming up short-cuts to get ahead. Unfortunately, the short-cuts almost always involve tricking other people or other unethical methods.

There are millions of people in the world, and *most folks have an average of two close friends* at any given time. So there's no need to settle for so-called friends who will just bring you down. You'll feel better by spending time with a special friend who is like you: thoughtful, considerate, kind, and honest.

One other thing: If you can maintain a positive mood, you're more apt to attract and keep positive-minded friends.

Avoiding Undue Stress

You've probably learned by now that there are some things in life you can control, and some that you can't. For example, you can control what you say to others, but you can't really control what they say back to you. You can't control which day your teacher schedules a pop quiz, but you can control being prepared through studying.

If you're under some stress right now—let's say you're studying for a big final exam—it's best to avoid taking on anything else that's stressful in your life for the time being, if possible. Keep life simple, simple, simple while you're focusing on a big project. This helps your ability to study and concentrate, thus increasing your self-confidence and self-esteem.

Life Balance

Even though you have a lot of important things to do, it's still important to have fun or play on a regular basis. Remember the phrase, "All work and no play makes Jane a dull girl?" It's true!

There's always time to inject a little fun into a busy day. So call a friend! Buy a new cassette tape! Go to the park and swing! Even a ten-minute time-out will give you a refreshing energy lift that will actually increase your effectiveness in studying and homework.

Give of Yourself

This is an often overlooked, yet very effective, way to instantly enhance your self-esteem: Give something to someone. You'll feel like one of Santa's elves when you see the look of pleasure and surprise on others' faces. Here are some suggestions:

✿ Donate your old clothes or toys to a charitable foundation.

✿ Go to a convalescent or retirement home and spend time making new friends. The elderly residents will love you for it.

✿ Volunteer to help a cause that you believe in (such as collecting donated clothes for a domestic violence shelter, feeding the homeless, or building a new church).

✿ Do a good deed for a neighbor, such as mowing her lawn for free.

PHYSICAL FITNESS

A fit body is more apt to feel "up" than a body that is out of shape. So make an investment in your positive self-image by getting plenty of exercise, fresh air, sleep, as well as having a good diet.

MANAGE YOUR ANGER

Everyone gets angry from time to time. Even though societal pressures tell females to "grin and bear it" instead of expressing anger, don't you believe it! Holding in anger leads to bigger problems, such as lowered concentration abilities or a bitter personality. On the other hand, it's not a good idea to go around telling people off, or punching them in the nose.

Several studies conclude that the **BEST ways to reduce anger are:**

1. **Talking** about your feelings with a parent, trusted friend, teacher, or school counselor.

2. **Writing** how you feel in a private diary or journal.

3. Physical **exercise**, including running, walking, or sports.

The WORST ways to decrease anger are:

1. **Hitting** something or somebody.

2. **Screaming**, especially at the person with whom you're angry.

3. **Holding anger in**, hoping it will go away.

Not only are these three methods ineffectual, but they can actually increase the amount of rage a person feels inside. So, the next time you feel your cheeks start to flush from anger, do yourself (and everyone around you) a favor and call a friend, go for a walk, or pound out your feelings with a pen on paper!

You CAN
Deal With It!

• •

: This chapter is filled with activities for building up good feel-
: ings about yourself. So now what? Share those ideas with a
: friend!

CHAPTER 13

You Have the Right to Your Feelings

Last week my mom accused me of making a mess that I know my little brother did. It made me mad and it hurt my feelings. Usually, I slam my bedroom door to show her I'm mad. But this time, I told my mom I didn't make the mess. And she listened to me and actually apologized for accusing me! Can you believe it?!

— Jade Luicas, age 13, Fremont, California

You've probably discovered some wonderful things about yourself in reading this book, such as:

❀ Every human being has feelings.

❀ Your feelings are normal and explainable.

❀ You have the right to your feelings, even if others don't understand or agree.

❀ Behind your feelings are valuable insights and information that can help you make the best decisions.

❀ Your changing moods are often triggered by your transition into young adulthood. It's normal to feel confused or awkward as your body, social life, and family relationships change.

❀ Your interests are changing, too. The things that fascinated you two years ago seem silly and childish today. Now that you're more grown up, you are noticing things related to adulthood: dating, getting ready for college, making money, friendships, and how you look.

❀ You may be experiencing pressure from many sources: friends, boys, teachers, and parents. Your transition into adulthood will be made smoother by you being aware of your values about right and wrong behavior, and plans for dealing with peer pressures.

❀ You can take steps that dramatically reduce your negative emotions, and increase your positive emotions. These include taking good care of your body and trying to keep your thoughts—especially about yourself—positive.

Your Emotions, Yourself

Feelings are a part of growing older, and a part of being human. We can't make emotions go away, but we can take steps to understand and manage them. With a little determination and effort on your part, you'll enjoy the countless experiences that are yet to come.

So have fun, laugh a lot, and enjoy your old and new friendships. In these small but important ways, you'll have the time of your life!

$\mathcal{G}$ LOSSARY

affirmations (af-fur-MAY-shuns): Positive words and sentences (such as "I am a good person") that affirm your self-worth, or which confirm your success in a situation (i.e., "I will easily pass my math exam"). Affirmations must be read, spoken, or written repeatedly for at least thirty days, to change a thinking habit from negative to positive.

aggressive (ah-GRESS-iv): Behavior or words that display a lack of respect for other's feelings or rights.

amino acid (ah-MEEN-oh a-SID): A basic building block of protein. Amino acids in protein foods, such as dairy products and meat, can alter moods or energy levels.

anorexia nervosa (a-no-REX-ee-ah nur-VOH-saw): A psychological and behavioral disorder marked by an unwillingness to eat sufficient foods for proper nourishment. Anorexia nervosa is an eating disorder which, if not properly treated, can lead to serious illness or death.

anxiety (ang-ZI-ih-tee): Worry and nervousness, often way out of proportion to the situation. Chronic anxiety often requires professional mental health treatment.

assertive (ah-SUR-tiv): Behavior and words that show respect for everybody's rights, opinions, and feelings—including your own.

binge-eating: The rapid consumption of large amounts of food, usually high-calorie snack foods.

block: A thought or belief which interferes with the attainment of happiness or a desired goal.

body image: How you feel about your body's shape and appearance. Also, the accuracy of your opinion about your body size and weight.

bulimia nervosa (bull-E-ME-ah nur-VOH-sah): A psychological and behavioral disorder marked by binge-eating, followed by purging behavior (exercise, laxatives, skipping meals, or vomiting) to rid the body of calories. Bulimia nervosa (also known as "bulimia," which means "appetite of an ox") rarely results in a low body weight; however, the purging can lead to deadly imbalances in electrolytes or suicidal behavior.

de-identification (dee-EYE-dent-if-ah-CAY-shun): Purposely deciding to act completely the opposite of another person, often a brother or a sister.

depression: An emotional condition marked by sadness, crying, and negative thoughts. Clinical depression, marked by chronic depression, as well as changes in sleeping or eating and/or thoughts about suicide, is a serious psychological condition warranting professional mental health or medical intervention.

distorted body image: Believing your body is much heavier, thinner, or less attractive than it really is.

dream journaling: The practice of writing down your previous night's dreams.

eating disorder: A psychological and behavioral problem centered around excessive concern about body weight and eating. Can involve skipping meals, binge-eating and/or purging. Can also be health or life-threatening, and require qualified intervention.

electrolytes (ee-LEKT-trowl-ites): Chemicals that conduct electrical charges in the brain. When these chemicals are depleted by the unhealthful behaviors of an eating disorder, severe health problems or even death can result.

hormones (HOR-mohnz): A wide variety of protein molecules that are produced and released from special glands in your body. Hormonal fluctuations associated with menstruation can create mood swings.

journaling: The practice of privately writing one's honest thoughts and feelings. Journaling is a highly effective way of resolving confusion and reducing negative emotions.

passive-aggressive (PAS-iv ah-GRESS-iv): Describes a communication style whereby a person says "yes" but then behaves as if she really wanted to say "no."

premenstrual syndrome: Also known as PMS. A set of physical and psychological changes and problematic symptoms created from the menstrual cycle. These can include irritability, swollen breasts, cramps, and lower back pain.

psychiatrist (si-KI-ih-TRIST): A professional trained to treat emotional and psychological disorders who is also a medical doctor licensed to prescribe drug treatments.

psychologist (si-CALL-uh-JIST): A professional trained to treat emotional and psychological disorders but not licensed to prescribe drugs.

purging (PERJ-ing): Action designed to rid the body of calories, including skipping meals, exercising, laxative use, and forced vomiting. These behaviors can result in health or life-threatening deficiencies in electrolytes.

self-esteem: The amount of positive or negative opinions and feelings one has about one's self. Also called self-image or self-concept.

separation-individuation (sep-ar-A-shun in-de-VID-you-a-shun): The process of letting go of childhood dependencies and becoming an independent adult.

serotonin (sair-uh-TON-in): A neurotransmitter (brain chemical) responsible for regulating mood and energy levels. Serotonin is affected by lifestyle habits, including diet, exercise, stress, and sleep.

unassertive (uhn-us-URT-iv): Not standing up for your own rights or feelings. Caving in to the demands of others at your own expense.

visualization (VIZH-you-ahl-iz-a-shun): Picturing your desires, aspirations, and goals in your mind's eye as a way of increasing confidence, faith, and determination.

Hotlines

If you or someone you know is in trouble, don't go it alone. Free, confidential help is just a phone call away. Most of these hotlines have toll-free numbers, so there's no reason not to reach out if you know you need help. Here are some hotlines staffed by trained counselors who can provide comfort, referrals to local professionals, and information.

NOTE: In cases of imminent physical trauma, danger, or suicidal behavior, dial 911 or 0 for immediate assistance.

SUICIDE PREVENTION HOTLINES

National Runaway and Suicide Hotline
1-800-621-4000
Provides 24-hour crisis intervention and referrals.

Kid Save
1-800-543-7283
Provides 24-hour crisis intervention and referrals for all mental health issues related to children and young adults.

SUBSTANCE ABUSE HOTLINE

National Institute of Drug Abuse
Parklawn Building, 5600 Fishers Lane, Room 10A-39
Rockville, MD 20852
1-800-662-4357
Provides 24-hour crisis counseling, referrals, and information related to alcoholism or substance abuse.

Covenant House Hotline
1-800-999-9999
Provides 24-hour crisis intervention and referrals, especially for young people who have or who are considering running away from home.

SEXUAL ASSAULT HOTLINES

Rape, Abuse, and Incest National Network (RAIN)
252 10th St. NE
Washington, DC 20002
1-800-656-4673 (HOPE)
This 24-hour hotline automatically connects you to a counselor near to you.

Child Help, USA
6463 Independence Ave.
Woodland Hills, CA 91367
1-800-422-4453 (1-800-4-A-CHILD)
A 24-hour hotline, referral, and information center specializing in child abuse and sexual crimes against children.

Sexual Assault Victims Hotline
1520 Eighth Ave.
Meridan, MI 39302
1-800-643-6250
This 24-hour hotline provides counseling and local referrals.

REFERRAL AGENCIES

The purpose of these agencies is to refer you to a local group or counselor who can help you. Usually, these agencies are not equipped to give crisis counseling over the telephone. Many of these referral centers provide mental health information, pamphlets, or reports that can be mailed to you free of charge.

CHILD ABUSE AND DOMESTIC VIOLENCE REFERRAL AGENCIES

National Organization for Victims Assistance (NOVA)
1757 Park Road NW
Washington, DC 20010
1-800-879-6682 (1-800-TRY-NOVA)
Provides 24-hour referrals, and victims' rights information for anyone who is a victim of a crime, including child abuse, domestic violence, and sexual assault.

National Victims Center
2111 Wilson Blvd., Suite 300
Arlington, VA 22201
1-800-394-2255 (1-800-FYI-CALL)
Provides referrals to local domestic violence shelters, open 9 to 5 Eastern Standard Time.

EATING DISORDERS REFERRAL AGENCIES

Renfrew Eating Disorder Center
1-800-RENFREW
Provides 24-hour referrals to local eating disorder treatment centers.

The American Anorexia / Bulimia Association
(212) 501-8351
Provides referrals to local eating disorder therapists, as well as general information.

The National Association of Anorexia Nervosa and Associated Disorders
(847) 831-3438
Provides referrals to local eating disorder therapists, as well as general information.

MENTAL HEALTH REFERRAL AGENCIES

National Alliance for the Mentally Ill
2101 Wilson Blvd., Suite 302
Arlington, VA 22201
1-800-950-6264
Makes referrals to local support groups and counselors.

National Foundation for Depressive Illness
P.O. Box 2257
New York, NY 10116
1-800-248-4344
Makes referrals to local organizations and counselors specializing in treating depression.

National Mental Health Association
1021 Prince St.
Alexandria, VA 22314
1-800-969-6642
Makes referrals to local support groups and counselors.

SUBSTANCE ABUSE REFERRAL AGENCIES

Alcoholics Anonymous
General Service Office
475 Riverside Drive
New York, NY 10115
Call directory assistance for the Alcoholic's Anonymous nearest you, or call (212) 870-3400 for referrals and information related to alcoholism.

COCAINE ABUSE REFERRAL AGENCIES

Cocaine Anonymous
1-800-347-8998
Provides 24-hour referrals and information related to cocaine abuse and addiction.

National Cocaine Abuse Hotline
1-800-COCAINE
Provides 24-hour referrals and information related to cocaine abuse and addiction.

INDEX

$\mathcal{A}$BOUT THE AUTHOR

Doreen Virtue, Ph.D., is a psychotherapist and former director of an adolescent mental health center and an all-women psychiatric hospital. She is the author of several self-help books about emotions, including the best-selling *Losing Your Pounds of Pain*. She is also a recipient of the Soroptomist Organization's "Women Helping Women" award. Dr. Virtue has appeared on many talk shows, including *Oprah, Montel, Geraldo, Donahue,* and *Sally Jesse Raphael*. Her work and writing have been featured in *McCall's, Woman's Day, YM, 'Teen, Sassy, New Body, Shape, T.V. Guide,* and *Vegetarian Times* magazines. The mother of two teenage sons, Dr. Virtue and her family live in Newport Beach, California.